Land Use – UK

A SURVEY FOR THE 21st CENTURY

Land Use – UK

A SURVEY FOR THE 21st CENTURY

edited by Rex Walford

A Survey for the 21st Century

THE GEOGRAPHICAL ASSOCIATION

Acknowledgements

The Geographical Association would like to thank the following people and organisations, without whose generous help the Land Use – UK project could not have been completed:

The 1400 schools (plus a sprinkling of other groups) and over 50,000 volunteer surveyors, for their time, effort and expertise. The schools and other groups are listed in full in Appendix 2.

Russell Chapman, for organising the Geographical Task Force

Crayola, who supplied the packs of coloured pencils for the survey at a much-reduced cost

The Dennis Curry Charitable Trust, the Ernest Cook Trust, the Frederick Soddy Trust, the Ordnance Survey, the Natural Environment Research Council and the Field Studies Council, for their financial assistance

Robin Fuller, Colin Barr and Sue Wallis of the Institute of Terrestrial Ecology, and Philip Kivell of the University of Keele, for their expert advice and support

John Halocha, for making the video of the project

Ralph and Marie Hebden, for allocating the squares, and Mo Morron, Pat Partington and Diane Wright, for matching up the 'twinned' schools

The Institute of Terrestrial Ecology research station at Monks Wood, Huntingdon, for accommodating the Results Team

Chris Kington, for expert advice on copyright and publishing matters

The Land Use – UK National Steering Committee, which comprised Mike Morrish (Chair), Rex Walford (Secretary), Liz Ambrose, Russell Chapman, David Cooper, Chris Durbin, Bob May, Mo Morron, Catherine St Ville, Geoffrey Sherlock and Julia Legg (ex-officio)

Julia Legg at GA Headquarters in Sheffield, and the temporary staff both at Sheffield and Monks Wood – Jonathan Taffs, Sara Smith, Avril Lawrence, Katy George, Heather Silvester and Tonny Olesen – for administering the project

The Ordnance Survey, for the gift of a 1:10000 map for each survey team which undertook the survey of a key square

The Results Team – David Cooper, Richard Dilley, Matthew Judd, Rob Lodge, Joan Lowdon, John McKeown, Mike Morrish, Catherine St Ville, Rex Walford and Anne Williams

The Royal Geographical Society with the Institute of British Geographers, the Scottish Association of Geography Teachers, the Royal Scottish Geographical Society and the Association of Geography Teachers in Wales, for their co-operation and support.

Edited by White Line Publishing Services
Index by Margaret Binns
Designed by Ledgard Jepson Ltd
Printed and bound in England by Butler and Tanner

ISBN 1 899085 31 9
First published 1997
Impression number 10 9 8 7 6 5 4 3 2 1
Year 2000 1999 1998 1997
Published by the Geographical Association, 343 Fulwood Road, Sheffield S10 3BP.
The Geographical Association is a registered charity: no 313129

Contents

List of contributors

The following people made major contributions to this book, producing them in a very short time; their work, and therefore this book, is based on the results generated by the thousands of Land Use – UK surveyors far too numerous to mention by name here, but whose institutions are listed in Appendix 2.

Colin Barr is Project Leader of the Department of the Environment Countryside Surveys at the Institute of Terrestrial Ecology, Merlewood Research Station, Cumbria

Tony Binns is Senior Lecturer in Geography at the University of Sussex and a Past President of the Geographical Association

Professor Alice Coleman, formerly of King's College, London, directed the Second Land Utilisation Survey during the 1960s

Frances Francis is Head of Geography at Braeside School for Girls, Buckhurst Hill, Essex

Robin Fuller is Head of the Remote Sensing Unit at the Institute of Terrestrial Ecology, Monks Wood, Huntingdon

Philip Kivell is Senior Lecturer in Geography at the University of Keele

Jeremy Krause is Senior Adviser – Geography for Cheshire County Council and an Honorary Secretary of the Geographical Association

Jon May is Lecturer in Geography in the School of Cultural and Community Studies at the University of Sussex

Mike Morrish is Head of Geography at Haberdashers' Aske's School for Boys, Elstree, Hertfordshire, and was President of the Geographical Association 1995–96

Moreen Morron is Headteacher at Harthill Primary School, Cheshire

Paula Richardson is a curriculum consultant in Surrey and formerly Adviser for Geography and History for Surrey County Council

Simon Rycroft is Lecturer in Geography in the School of Cultural and Community Studies at the University of Sussex

Rex Walford is Lecturer in Geography and Education at the University of Cambridge, a Fellow of Wolfson College, Cambridge, and a Past President of the Geographical Association

Dr Edward Christie Willatts was Organising Secretary of the First Land Utilisation Survey from 1931 to 1942; he retired from his post as Principal Planner at the Department of the Environment in 1973

In addition to the main contributors, we should also like to thank the many people who kindly sent in photographs and other illustrations to illustrate the book. Wherever possible, we have credited the photographer beside each photograph.

Foreword

I am delighted to introduce this book. It celebrates the 1996 Land Use – UK survey and sets out its origins and organisation, the results, an analysis and interpretation of the data, the experiences of the surveyors, some reflections on the exercise, and its historic context.

Land Use – UK was an endeavour on an heroic scale. To conceive and carry through an enterprise of such dimensions, relying largely on voluntary help, at such remarkable speed, was a singular achievement. It was an immense undertaking, and the success of Land Use – UK owes much to the courage, vision, initiative and energy of Rex Walford, Mike Morrish and the National Steering Committee.

One major success of the project has been in mobilising the enthusiasm of so many people in various aspects of the survey. Teachers and pupils at all levels, staff and students in higher education, Geographical Association officers and staff, people and organisations who provided financial help – around 50,000 people in all made vital contributions to the survey. Their efforts have culminated in this unique snapshot of the UK in 1996 – a project of enormous geographical, environmental and educational value which adds substantially to our understanding of our land and the way we use it. I have no hesitation in recommending it to you.

W. Ashley Kent
President of the Geographical Association 1996–97

Photo: Peter Hoare

*Charterhouse School
pupils showing Her
Majesty the Queen the
results of their Land
Use-UK survey*

Introduction

Land Use – UK was 'a remarkable achievement' according to the Department of the Environment and a 'wonderful experience' according to hundreds of teachers and pupils. The mobilisation of nearly 1500 schools and 50,000 pupils in the summer of 1996, allied to expert help, computer analysis and much voluntary endeavour in administration, has combined to create an experience which has not only had a profound educational impact but has also contributed to the nation's environmental database. Perhaps even more significantly, it revealed as never before the environmental views, visions and concerns of the generation which will inherit the stewardship of the United Kingdom in the twenty-first century.

This book has been compiled with three major intentions:

- to record the aims, objectives, events and experiences that led to the Land Use – UK survey organised by the Geographical Association in the summer of 1996
- to put the preliminary results of the survey into the public domain, along with analysis and commentary
- to provide some perspective about the survey and its intentions, through evaluation, reflection, and a consideration of past land-use surveys.

Many readers will be those who took part at the 'chalk-face' of Land Use – UK, who will primarily want to read about the wider picture of which they were a part. Their experiences are recorded in Parts 1 and 3, and they carry a heartening echo of a task both challenging and enjoyed. I hope they will also derive some satisfaction from seeing their school or organisation listed in the roll of honour in Appendix 2.

Others may be enthusiasts or campaigners in the environmental field who are anxious to test their perceptions or confirm their own opinions by reference to the results presented in Part 2. Some striking features leap out, such as the doubling of the area of woodland since 1930, the tiny amount of urban land now occupied by industry, the perception of 'traffic' as our major environmental problem, and young people's depressing vision of our urban future. Much more remains to be ascertained from further analytical work on the immense and rich database which has been gathered, if only funds can be found to finance it.

A third set of readers will be those in academic life: if geographers, their field of study may be the UK in particular, or the environment in general; if educationalists, their interests may lie in the politics of the curriculum or the role of professional subject-associations. From these perspectives Land Use – UK may variously be seen as an exciting crusade about environmental awareness and citizenship, a thorough piece of data-collection, or as an interesting episode of its time engineered for a variety of motives. For this audience the reflective and historical chapters in Parts 4 and 5 may hold most interest.

The contributors responded nobly to the editor's call for urgency, to produce the book within a few months of the project's conclusion. Thus, it is unlikely that this will be the final word on Land Use – UK, or a dispassionate one. Some may want to take the book as a starting-point, as evidence to tease out further the issues surrounding the nature, organisation and findings of the project and to evaluate Land Use – UK in other contexts. However, some things are certain. For those caught up in the project during the last three years, it has been an exciting and heartening experience. In the midst of an era supposedly marked by minimalist attitudes and low morale in schools, Land Use – UK has proved a shot in the arm, a tonic, an eye-opener. To a generation of teachers overwhelmed by bureaucracy and administration it has literally been 'a breath of fresh air'. It has also demonstrated quite clearly the incomparable value of fieldwork and geography in a properly rounded school education.

Rex Walford Cambridge, January 1997

Photo: Chris Garnett

Chapter 1:
The origins of the survey

Rex Walford and Mike Morrish

In the summer of 1996 groups of school pupils (and a few others besides) could be found all over the United Kingdom attentively scanning the landscape or townscape, with clipboards and pencils at the ready. They ranged from classes in infant schools zealously shepherded and advised by their teachers, to intrepid sixth-form groups on Duke of Edinburgh Award expeditions. They were tramping over isolated highland moors and through populated urban neighbourhoods, through leafy rural lanes and desolated inner-city areas. They were taking part in what one national newspaper eye-catchingly dubbed 'the largest geography lesson in the world': the Land Use – UK survey.

The survey, organised by the Geographical Association, had emerged as a major project after two years of discussion and planning, though the influences on its genesis can be traced back over a much longer period.

Concern for geography in the National Curriculum

A major influence was concern for the curriculum position of geography in British schools – a concern which stretched back to the first attempts by the government to tiptoe into the 'secret garden' of the curriculum in the early 1970s. In the intervening period, the Geographical Association had learned to become pro-active on the subject's behalf. Alert campaigning, allied to skilful negotiation and presentation, had helped geography to find a place in the 'broad and balanced curriculum' proposed by Kenneth Baker in 1988 when a National Curriculum was first mooted. However, the welcome prospect of it being studied by all pupils between the ages of 5 and 16 was undone by later revisions overseen by Sir Ron Dearing. The disputed events and accounts of that turbulent period still need to be fully untangled, but there is no doubt about the unanimous disappointment with which geographers greeted the 1994 decision to remove their subject from the list of those which were to be mandatory at key stage 4 (broadly speaking, for pupils aged between 14 and 16).

Rhetoric about the value of geography was a satisfying response, but the listeners tended to be only those who agreed with the proposition in the first place. Lobbying government officials and ministers seemed more relevant, but it was comparatively ineffective without access to the one or two real opinion-formers. The idea quickly crystallised that geographers would do better to seek a **practical** demonstration of the inherent worth and value of their subject in schools on a grand scale. In this way, despite competing curriculum initiatives and attractions, there would be an opportunity to bring it to the notice of parents, governors and the general public, through a special event.

Once this idea had begun to attract broad support, it was not surprising that, following the Dearing revisions, discussion moved to the idea of showing geography's interest and challenge through mass involvement in a high-profile piece of fieldwork – an activity which had been embedded deep into British school geography as far back as the 1930s. Many teachers preserved the belief that fieldwork was elemental to the study of the subject, and the renewed emphasis on place studies, engendered through the National Curriculum debate on geography, provided a helpful spur to this. Though the National Curriculum Working Group had failed in their endeavour to get 'residential fieldwork in an unfamiliar environment' written into the subject's blueprint, there was a written requirement for fieldwork of some kind, even in the later truncated specification produced by the School Curriculum and Assessment Authority.

The influence of Local Agenda 21

Curriculum matters were by no means the only circumstances which had led towards the development of the Land Use – UK project. There was an important conference about the environment at Rio de Janeiro in 1992, which was attended by many national leaders. This increased the concern about the quality of stewardship which the world was exercising. A number of well-publicised proposals from the Rio conference went echoing around the globe in the months and years following it, and one of the more practical of these was Local Agenda 21. This is a call for increased study and understanding by young people of their own local environments. The implementation of Local Agenda 21 by geography teachers had been a matter of interest to the Geographical Association, but the idea of Land Use – UK transformed it into a practical intention.

A transatlantic example

A third influence came from activities in the USA. In the early 1980s, geography there was almost down and out as a separate subject in the school curriculum, mostly subsumed in social studies and taught only to a few pupils for a single year in high school. The quality of students and teachers alike was poor. But the organisation of a national Geography Awareness Week in 1987 – promulgated in Congress and actively promoted and financially supported by the National Geographic Society – began to turn the tide.

The Week had continued annually, with each having a theme such as 'reflections on water', 'cities', 'the wilderness' and 'passport to the world'. The initial disaster scenario about American children's ignorance of geography was progressively replaced with more positive and upbeat statements about the value of the subject. The American experience of Geography Awareness Week seemed to demonstrate the virtues of co-ordinating and highlighting events for a short designated period of time.

The Geographical Association had drawn attention to the phenomenon of the USA Geography Awareness Week at the Council of British Geography's autumn meeting in 1992, and had asked why something similar should not be organised in the UK. However, the response from representatives of higher-education bodies was mixed, perhaps because geography was not then seen as being under challenge in higher education to the extent that it was in schools. So the idea of a concerted national event or campaign by all geographical bodies was diplomatically put on a back burner and the matter referred back to the GA, who were thought to be the organisation most likely to be interested in pursuing it further.

The GA Council had examined the American example and concluded that the idea of an Action Week demonstrating the current strengths of the subject would be more appropriate than that of an Awareness Week, which seemed based on an acknowledgement of the subject's weakness in schools. But it was still debating the merits or otherwise of attaching a theme to such an event when the idea of a land-use survey came into view. This immediately appealed as a suitable focus – although subsequent deliberation modified the intention so that it was the results of the survey, rather than the survey itself, which became a component of the designated Week.

An article appears

Prompted by all these influences an idea was emerging. But it was to be another event, a fortuitously timed publication, which was to be the stimulus that caused the project to take its eventual shape and form.

In the summer of 1994 the *Geographical Journal* published an article by three scientists from the Institute of Terrestrial Ecology, a research institute which is funded by the Natural Environment Research Council to carry out studies of the countryside. The article was timed to coincide with the publication of the ITE's new *Land Cover Map of Britain*, derived from images created by remote sensing. Its authors, Colin Barr, Robin Fuller and John Sheail, compared contemporary data with that produced by the Land Utilisation Survey of the 1930s, a nationwide initiative organised by one of Britain's best-known geographers, L. Dudley Stamp.

Land-use survey had scarcely been noticed as a geographical area of interest for more than a decade, but the members of the small GA group deputed to consider a possible Action Week realised that here they might have found the essential component that they had been searching for.

The article was generous in its assessment of Stamp's pioneering work of more than sixty years ago. That survey had mapped the land uses of Britain comprehensively for the first time, thanks to the indefatigable efforts of Stamp himself and Dr E. C. Willatts, the Secretary (see Chapter 17), as well as to the generosity of some trusts, the support of the LSE (where Stamp lectured) and, certainly not least, the noble efforts of more than ten thousand schools and an estimated 250,000 school pupils.

A comparable land-use survey in the 1990s would not only be a vehicle for clear educational benefits such as the exercise of field-observation skills and the use of mapping techniques, but it could combine tried-and-tested fieldwork activity with modern work in the sphere of information technology, especially if the results were recorded and transmitted by computer.

A land-use survey would also link back directly to a tradition in which pupils had played an important part. Schools had formed the backbone of the Stamp survey in the 1930s, and had taken part again in the 1960s when one of Stamp's younger colleagues, Professor Alice Coleman, had organised the second national Land Utilisation Survey (see Chapter 18).

Now, another thirty years on, was the time perhaps ripe for the resource of schools to be mobilised again? If so, there would need to be a careful consideration of objectives within the new context; there would be little to be gained in repeating an exercise for the sake of nostalgia.

Taking shape

The idea quickly took shape and was greeted with enthusiasm by the first GA groups which considered it; more importantly Barr, Fuller and Sheail at the ITE, when approached, were positive about co-operating. Although much of their own work was with satellite images, they recognised the continuing importance of verifying image data by field-survey, and kept survey teams in the field themselves. They welcomed the chance of supplementary data being generated by a GA-organised survey, as long as the methods of collection were properly rigorous and scientific.

Among the ITE's most recent work had been the Countryside Survey of 1990 and the development of the Countryside Information System (CIS). The CIS is a geographic information program used by government departments, with only limited availability in the public domain. The use of the CIS was offered for the analysis of the data which the GA survey would generate.

From the GA's point of view, the link to the ITE was of great benefit. The survey, besides having credibility as a valuable educational exercise, could now also contribute to the national database of environmental information which was being established. School pupils would have the satisfaction and pride of knowing that their own efforts were destined to be used for the nation's ultimate good and not merely filed away in a departmental stock-cupboard.

But the ITE's work concentrated on rural landscapes, and although about 90% of the UK land is rural in character, 90% of the population lives in urban areas. It was the view of the GA National Steering Committee that any survey of the 1990s needed to encompass both facets of the nation's character. So the help of a leading academic geographer was sought who was an expert on urban land-use. Philip Kivell of the University of Keele is well known in this field, and in November 1994 he accepted the invitation to join Colin Barr and Robin Fuller in devising the basis of a major survey which was now formally given the title 'Land Use – UK'.

Links to the past?

Whereas the Stamp and Coleman surveys had attempted to map every parcel of land in England and Wales, plus all or part of Scotland, it was now recognised that a stratified sampling approach could produce accurate generalised data. There was no longer any need to cover every piece of land in order to determine national and regional land use with a high degree of accuracy. So, using classifications already developed by the ITE, a unique stratified sample of 1029 'key squares' was set up, each of 1 square kilometre. This is described in more detail in Chapter 2.

One central task of the 1996 survey would obviously be the mapping of these squares and the classification of the land according to different uses, followed by a calculation of the percentages of land given over to each use. But what classification should be used? If the categories were based on either of the earlier surveys, some comparisons might be made; on the other hand, given the lessons learned from those surveys and the changing landscape context, it might prove to be unnecessarily restricting if we simply followed the patterns of the past.

Stamp had used a very basic framework of seven categories, arguing that the classification needed to be applied readily and easily by surveyors with limited experience. By contrast, the Coleman survey had used an elaborate classification of 64 categories in its desire to record accurately the variety of different crop and vegetation types. There was considerable discussion in the Land Use – UK Survey Design sub-committee about this matter.

The 1996 survey would be undertaken in a more urbanised landscape than its predecessors, so there was a desire to expand the urban categories and to have at least as many as there were in the rural classification. However, some survey teams would have squares of mixed landscape where both urban and rural categories would be found. At what level of complexity could survey teams reasonably work, given that they might be involved in both rural and urban classification – and given that the task had to be carried out with precision by pupils of diverse ages? The desirability of a detailed classification clashed with considerations of practicality and likely accuracy. In the end the Survey Design group decided that 20 was the 'golden number' within which the classification should be confined.

In June 1995 a pilot survey was undertaken by 17 schools, to check that the plans so far were workable in practice. An experiment to try to identify different types of housing density was made in the pilot survey, but the responses from the participating schools indicated that this was too much for the survey teams to handle. So, in the end, using the best advice available, 10 rural and 8 urban categories were specified, trialled and later described in some detail for the Survey Handbook (see Appendix 1). One further category was added for 'unsurveyed', and the twentieth was belatedly allocated to 'sea'.

Beyond the mapping

By recording land use, the 1996 UK survey was copying the work of Stamp and Coleman – even though it was recognised that the use of sample squares, as opposed to total coverage, limited the contextual and general information which could be gleaned. But on the other hand, Stamp's work had not covered Northern Ireland at all, and his survey had taken several years to complete. Similarly Coleman's survey work had been spread through almost a decade and had covered neither Northern Ireland nor the highland areas of Scotland. Although the scale of operation was not so enormous, at least with the sample-square approach all parts of the United Kingdom could be covered, and the attempt would be made to complete the survey within a twelve-week period (June–August 1996).

Special interests

The Survey Design group had a strong desire to go beyond the straightforward repetition of past methods. Both the study of geography and the state of the environment had altered over 60 years, and it was thought important to benefit from all relevant new insights.

The growth (or decline) of particular landscape and townscape features and their impact on localities and communities was signalled as being of particular interest by the responses from teachers involved in the pilot survey and sundry campaigning organisations who contacted the GA when they heard that the survey was going to take place. Another early concern was the supposed disappearance of hedgerows, but as there were great practical difficulties in identifying exactly what was and was not included in the term, it was reluctantly not included as a feature of the project.

It was clear that both teachers and pupils wanted to explore the high-profile issue of whether new housing was eating up open space, and bodies such as the Council for the Protection of Rural England also urged that this topic be considered. Similarly, as a result of many requests, the supposed disappearance of village and corner shops was included.

It was thought much more difficult, however, to ask surveyors to pronounce on matters of quality (e.g. what would be 'sub-standard housing' or 'poorly maintained roads') and, however interesting or relevant these questions were, they were excluded on practical grounds. The glory of a large survey force also brings the constraint that the survey task must be clear and capable of being completed accurately by all the participants.

Mushrooming reports in the press about conflicts caused by the siting of new communications and satellite towers (often erected quickly through loopholes in planning legislation) led to the inclusion of that topic in what eventually became known as 'Task 2' or the 'national issues' section. The first thought was to mark these specific features on a separate map, but this eventually gave way to a simpler form of recording – noting the presence or absence of the features in the square under survey. Survey teams were nevertheless encouraged to write supplementary comments and descriptions about what they found, and many of them took the trouble to do so.

Views and visions

A further possible element of the project emerged, partly as a result of a correspondence with Professor Denis Cosgrove (who had published probing and questioning articles about the earlier Stamp survey) and partly through animated discussion within the Survey Design team, where those most concerned with the scientific data suggested that the survey should also turn the mirror on those who were doing the surveying. Cosgrove, in a friendly response to a letter seeking amplification of his reservations about the Stamp survey, had made this point to the Survey National Steering Committee:

> *Is there not a responsibility to 'guide' and 'lead', in the sense of developing the [surveyors'] critical and imaginative faculties towards visions of citizenship in the course of the survey?*

Photo: R W Saunders

Young surveyors, young citizens

The idea of 'guiding and leading' towards citizenship seemed problematic if not impractical, but the possibility of exploring the views of those doing the surveying quickly gained support from all sides. It was recognised that it would be timely and important to discover just how the present generation of school students view their own environments and what their perceptions of the future might be. In doing so, an insight into the extent and nature of their perceptions of immediate 'citizenship' would, in turn, be gained.

The survey designers also wondered if, despite the supposed 'greening' of politics, they would find any evidence to suggest that environmental issues are high on the agenda of the younger generation. Have we, as some activist groups optimistically suggest, a highly conscious teenage population who in general are increasingly concerned for environmental issues and consequences? Or might we discover that the vast majority of present-day school pupils live geographically as well as socially fragmented lives, that the world of technology increasingly gets in the way of an interest in the natural environment, and that affinity to a local community or landscape means little to them?

The introduction of a 'views and visions' section into the survey would allow students themselves to express views about the character and the environmental issues of the area they were surveying, as well as allowing us to gauge their views about the changes that they wanted to see. The response sheet was deliberately made free-form to encourage variety and diversity of expression, although it was recognised that this would require extra time and care in analysing the responses.

The three tasks

The survey design team had thus defined three major tasks for the surveyors:

Task 1: to map the sample squares and record their land use

Task 2: to record the occurrence in their squares of five specific types of feature or 'national issues' (see pages 53 and 59-60)

Task 3: after the fieldwork, to discuss and record their 'views and visions' for their area.

In the background

The autumn of 1995 was a crowded time as the various aspects of project preparation came together. Other groups were wrestling with logistics, administration and publicity. Without any paid staff devoted specifically to the project, the burden fell on GA headquarters and the volunteers of the National Steering Committee.

Behind it all lay cliff-hanging situations concerned with finance – a long, professionally conducted search for sponsorship, with some agonising near misses in obtaining major support, but ultimately no success. This demanded an emergency re-appraisal of the scale of the project. Contingency plans were devised by the score, and the GA Treasurer courageously underwrote the project when the financial situation was at its bleakest.

As 1996 approached, there was confidence in the thoroughness of the preparation but little certainty how the survey would turn out in practice ...

The objectives of Land Use – UK

1   To provide a contemporary picture of the land use of the United Kingdom through a survey undertaken in an extensive sample of one-kilometre grid squares, based on a stratified sample of both rural and urban landscapes

2   To further the intentions of Local Agenda 21 of the world environmental conference held at Rio de Janeiro in 1992, in which greater knowledge and understanding of the local environment was urged

3   To identify some local, regional and national issues concerning the current use of land in the United Kingdom

4   To discover the perceptions, views and future visions of primary and secondary school students concerning the environments which they were to survey

5   To provide data on land use in the United Kingdom in the 1990s which can be compared with the data from the land-use surveys carried out in the 1930s and 1960s

6   To emphasise the value of survey work as a preparation for citizenship

7   To give pupils the chance to develop and exercise observation, map, survey, recording and presentation skills as part of their school education

8   To give teachers the chance to demonstrate the interest, enjoyment and relevance of planned, task-oriented fieldwork as part of the educational experience

9   To give schools the chance to focus on geographical studies as a worthwhile and necessary part of the whole educational programme at all ages

10 To promote the objectives of the Geographical Association, a charitable body founded 'to further the study and teaching of geography'

These objectives were agreed by the Council of the Geographical Association.

Chapter 2: Devising the key sample

Colin Barr, Robin Fuller, Philip Kivell and Rex Walford

Background – sampling and recording

The two previous national land-use surveys in which school pupils had been involved had both sought to cover the British landscape comprehensively. In the case of the first survey, the whole of England, Wales and Scotland was covered by volunteer surveyors during a period of three or four years, and maps of all Britain were published at the one-inch scale. Some of the original field maps and plates of the printed maps were destroyed by bombing during the air-raids on London in the Second World War, but full sets of the printed maps can be located in major libraries. Eventually county memoirs were written by various authors, and in 1948 Dudley Stamp published his summary volume, *The Land of Britain: its use and misuse.*

For the second survey the whole of England and Wales was covered, as well as parts of Scotland. All the field maps are still in existence, but only a small proportion of them were turned into printed maps (2½-inch scale) because of the high cost of colour printing and the lack of funding in the 1960s and 1970s. No county memoirs were produced, although Professor Coleman did publish a comprehensive 50-page article about the survey in the 19 January 1977 issue of *The Architects Journal.*

For Land Use – UK in 1996, an early decision had to be made about how far the pattern of the past should be followed. The National Steering Committee decided that, although it wanted to generate national and regional pictures of land use for comparison with the earlier surveys, the production of maps for every square kilometre of the kingdom would not be a part of the scheme. Enough had been learned about sampling procedures for results of considerable precision to be produced. A survey based on sampling would be of manageable proportions and would take far less time than a comprehensive survey.

It was recognised that it would be easier to complete the survey in England and Wales than in Scotland, where there were large areas remote from all human habitation, let alone schools. Even so, it was thought that, with careful use of sampling procedures, Scotland could be effectively covered. It was also decided to include Northern Ireland, so that this survey would be representative of the whole of the United Kingdom.

The question then arose of how best to organise the sample. It was known that the Institute of Terrestrial Ecology had been monitoring the countryside using a sample-based strategy since 1978 (see panel on page 21). Their system was based on one-kilometre squares which can easily be referenced and identified on standard Ordnance

Figure 2.1
The ITE Land
Classification
The colours on the
map represent the
32 classes devised
by ITE for the
rural landscape of
Britain. The Land
Use-UK sample
was stratified to
ensure a suitable
representation
from each of these
classes

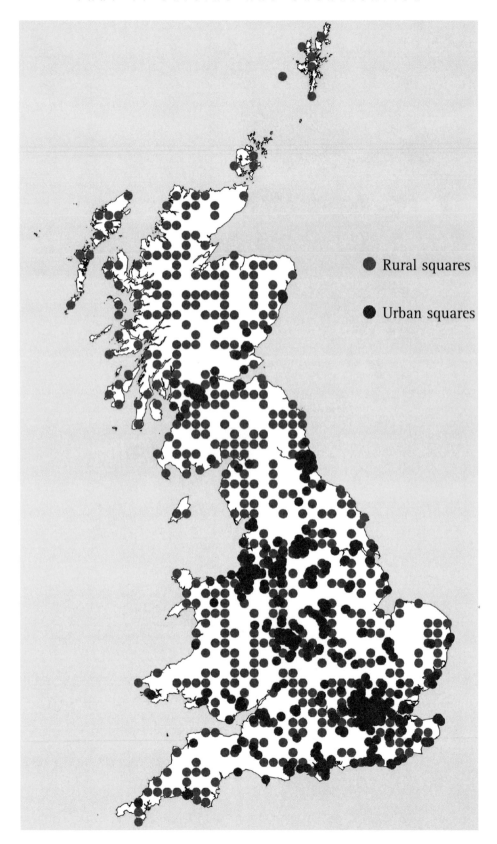

Figure 2.2
Key squares (excluding
Northern Ireland)

Survey maps. However, although the ITE sample was carefully stratified so that different landscape types are represented, it could not be used on its own for this survey because it deliberately excludes areas which are predominantly urban. For Land Use – UK to investigate the whole of the nation, there had to be a way of including the urban areas too.

In the mid-1970s the Institute of Terrestrial Ecology (ITE) developed a sample-based strategy for recording Britain's stock of countryside features. To ensure that the full range of land types was represented, the sampling programme divided Britain into 32 environmental classes of land, based on map information, which included climate, topography, geology and, in broad terms, geographical location. One-kilometre squares with more than 75% built-up land were excluded from this analysis and classified as predominantly urban. This system is known as the ITE Land Classification (see Fig 2.1).

In 1978, 1984 and 1990, the ITE conducted Countryside Surveys, during which a sample of between 8 and 24 one-kilometre squares in each of these ITE Land Classes was inspected. Field-recording included data on land cover, land use and landscape-management practices; it also included maps of linear features such as hedges and ditches, records of ponds and trees in open land, and detailed information on the plant species associated with all these various habitats.

Britain is highly urbanised, with approximately 90% of the population living on less than 10% of the land. An undifferentiated sample of grid squares randomly selected across the country would inevitably be biased towards rural land and would grossly under-represent the immediate living environment of the majority of the people. The decision was taken to use the ITE system for the rural land, but to add a significant number of squares from the urban land. There was also the subsidiary consideration that the distribution of the nation's schools closely mirrors that of the population, so most of them are in urban localities. Giving equal weighting to these urban areas would reduce transport and access problems for many of the surveyors.

Practical considerations were then weighed against statistical ones in deciding the size of the sample. The ITE had eventually used 508 rural squares for its stratified sample, although it had started with fewer. After considerable discussion Land Use – UK decided that a base of 500 rural squares and 500 urban ones would deliver reasonably accurate sampling in Britain. A further 29 squares were generated in the same way for Northern Ireland.

ITE's procedures allowed sample squares to be generated easily from the vast area of Britain that is not classified as 'predominantly urban'.

The rural sample

The Land Use – UK rural squares cover 97.4% of the landscape, similar to the area surveyed by ITE, but we chose a new sample set of one-kilometre squares. Rural land use was recorded in the 20 categories (see Appendix 1), marking the results directly onto Ordnance Survey 1:10000 map sheets. A grid of 10 x 10 points was then overlaid onto the map, and students estimated the proportions of the different categories using this sub-sample of 100 points, by counting the number of points in each category.

All the squares belonging to a single ITE Land Class were brought together in a spreadsheet and the average results calculated for each category in each Land Class. Because the squares in a class may have some differences in their land-use composition, it was also possible to calculate the statistical variance – a measure of the variability within an ITE Land Class.

We know the exact distribution throughout Britain of each ITE Land Class. We have estimated from the field surveys how, on average, their land use is made up. It is therefore possible to calculate national and regional estimates of land use, weighting the calculation according to the number of squares of each class. This was done automatically, using the Countryside Information System (see pages 13-14). This program also looked at the variances within the data and calculated the 'standard error' – a measure of how much confidence can be placed in the reliability of the estimates for each category. The regional estimates were based on the same standard regions as used for the urban classification (see Figure 2.3).

Urban squares

The densely built-up 2.6% of land not covered by the rural survey was treated as urban and sampled and surveyed separately. Land Use – UK's 500 urban squares were all from this area. Selecting them was not so simple.

There are a number of difficulties in selecting and mapping sample squares in urban areas, because there is no widely accepted scheme which categorises urban land or settlement types. A number of different surveys of land use, or land cover, have been undertaken in the past – see for example Kivell (1993) and Department of the Environment (1990) – but none of them provided an ideal base for the present purposes. It was also impossible to relate any of these schemes to the framework of one-kilometre grid squares that had been chosen for the present survey.

Another important consideration was that the rural and urban parts of the survey should develop from the same starting point and be broadly compatible. In order to ensure complete coverage of the country, with no overlap, it was necessary to draw the samples of urban and rural squares from the same universe. For this reason the ITE Land Classification was also used as the starting point for the urban surveys. ITE identify 6,320 squares that are more than 75% built-up, and Land Use – UK selected 500 of these at random, giving a sample close to 1 in 12.5. In all of the analyses in later chapters, it should be remembered that the data were collected on this sample basis by many different teams of surveyors, whose interpretation of some of the finer points will also have differed.

The reasons for undertaking separate urban and rural surveys have been outlined above, and the justification is largely a practical one. This separation should not be over-stressed, because the division is not always clear-cut, and some of the most contentious environmental and planning issues occur where urban and rural meet. Also, significant amounts of built-up development were found in the countryside – and, conversely, many urban areas were found to contain elements of woodland, tended open space and relatively undeveloped land surrounding public institutions. The results of the rural sample presented in Chapter 6 show that 7.6% of the rural landscape is actually built-up; if this is added to the 2.6% which is identified as predominantly urban, the survey indicates that around 10.2% of Britain is currently built-up.

At the initial stage of analysis, it is useful to say something about the whole set of urban squares, but it is also desirable to subdivide them for more detailed analysis. This has been done in two ways. First, there is a regional subdivision, based upon the standard English regions used for the 1991 Census (Office of Population Censuses and Surveys, 1991) plus Wales and Scotland, as tabulated in Figure 2.3. Northern Ireland is omitted as it does not form part of the remit of the Countryside Surveys or of ITE, and so the original data sets are for Britain only.

Figure 2.3
Regions used for analysis

1	North	6	South-West
2	Yorkshire/Humberside	7	West Midlands
3	East Midlands	8	North-West
4	East Anglia	9	Wales
5	South-East	10	Scotland

Secondly, in order to distinguish between urban settlements of broadly different types, we have used a classification recently produced by the Office for National

Statistics (ONS). Essentially this classification is a grouping of local authorities based upon 37 separate variables from the 1991 census. These are analysed in order to assign local authorities to one of 34 clusters, which are further grouped into twelve groups and six families. The families are tabulated in Figure 2.4.

Family no.	Name	Examples with surveyed squares
1	Rural areas	Harrogate, Perth and Kinross, Aberystwyth
2	Prospering areas	Poole, St Albans, Charnwood
3	Maturer areas	Hove, Redbridge, Aberdeen
4	Urban centres	Bristol, Northampton, Oldham
5	Mining and industrial	Inverclyde, Manchester, Merthyr Tydfil
6	Inner London	Ealing, Greenwich, Newham

Figure 2.4
ONS classification of local authorities into families

The ONS classification differs from the ITE rural classification in that it is not based upon land use or physical characteristics, and it does not use grid squares as its basic component. It is not possible to say definitively that grid square X belongs to, say, family 5 (mining and industrial); one can only say that grid square X is situated in a local authority district that is itself categorised as mining and industrial. If a grid square is divided between more than one local authority, it is deemed to belong to the authority in which the majority of its area lies.

One potential confusion that needs to be clarified here is that some of the urban squares are located in family 1 local authorities (rural areas). In fact this is not a contradiction because family 1 contains subdivisions with significant urban settlements. These include categories called 'towns in the country' (e.g. Yeovil) and 'industrial margins' (e.g. Crewe).

This classification scheme is useful for our purposes because it provides a broad context of settlement types within which the surveyed areas are contained.

Sampling and remote sensing

Many may ask how such survey techniques fit in with new methods of 'remote sensing' which use data recorded from Earth-observation satellites to record, map and measure the surface features. The simple answer is that sample-based field surveys and remote-sensing data are entirely complementary – indeed, in many studies they are inseparable. Remote sensing gives us a generalised overview and allows us to map a limited range of cover types. It can tell us very little about the finer detail – the land use, the stocking density, the plant species in fields, the animals associated with them, the hedgerows, trees and ponds of the landscape. Conversely, field survey cannot record all such details for large areas. However, by mapping the broad picture through remote sensing and by then adding the detail through field-based sampling, professional ecologists can combine large-area coverage with fine-resolution detail. The combination of these different techniques can prove much more valuable to the user than either one on its own.

Photo: Rex Walford

Marie and Ralph Hebden allocating squares at GA headquarters, spring 1996.

Chapter 3:
Organising the survey

Rex Walford

The launch

Land Use – UK was launched in January 1996 via all the Geographical Association's journals (*Geography*, *Teaching Geography* and *Primary Geographer*). Articles by members of the National Steering Committee explained the background to the survey, described the three Tasks, referred to the earlier surveys of Stamp and Coleman, and included a recruitment form to be completed and returned as soon as possible.

At that stage none of us really knew what level of response the articles would provoke. The gloomiest predictions suggested that the project might be one idea too far for hard-pressed teachers struggling in a morass of National Curriculum paperwork and new inspection and assessment arrangements. Another fear was that the proposed registration fee, necessary to overcome the lack of commercial sponsorship, would deter schools which would otherwise have participated.

The Survey Pack

In the curious lull before the first responses arrived, we busied ourselves by putting the finishing touches to the pack, the chief component of which was the Survey Handbook. The previous two surveys had issued small handbooks, but we had decided, after considerable thought, to issue the total of 44 pages of material in five separate colour-coded sections inside a sturdy wallet, so that they could easily be dismembered and photocopied. The sections of the Handbook were as follows:

1 Introductory

This included a basic description of the project, letters of support and encouragement from Dudley Stamp's son and from Alice Coleman, and poster-diagrams of the objectives.

2 Preparing for the survey – guidelines

This included practical suggestions and guidance for teachers on ways in which the survey could be organised, how to obtain the base map, what briefing might be necessary, etc. There was also advice about the health and safety factors which would have to be considered in fieldwork as far-ranging as this.

3 Doing the survey – documents for the surveyors

This section contained the instructions for doing the survey in the field and a comprehensive listing of the 19 (later 20) survey categories, with explanatory notes (see Appendix 1).

4 Presenting the results

This gave information about how to map the land uses by using the prescribed colours and recording the percentages. Instructions for doing this on paper and computer disk were provided. At one stage we had considered requiring all results to be returned on disk, but the assumption was that not all schools would yet have the knowledge or equipment to do this. As it turned out, providing the paper option was the correct decision, as many schools favoured this. When the results came in, only about one-fifth of the returns were on disk.

5 Background

We included a selection of background material, including a description and map of the key squares, information about the previous land-use surveys, sample letters to parents and landowners, suggestions for extra local activities, and notes on media and training opportunities.

Badges and crayons

In addition to the colour-coded sections, the pack included sheets of adhesive badges. These proclaimed **We're surveying for Land Use – UK**, and carried the attractive Land Use – UK logo in brown and green. The badges were to prove a highly effective and popular way of identifying the surveying teams and providing a degree of authority when dealing with farmers, landowners and the public generally.

Crayola supplied the essential coloured pencils at an advantageous price, and a set of these was included in every pack. Without these it would have been impossible to maintain the required degree of uniformity in the returns.

Confirmation form

The final item in the packs sent from the GA Headquarters was a form for schools to return to 'complete the contract' as soon as they had been offered a specific square.

Ordnance Survey maps

Through the generous co-operation of the Ordnance Survey, each school undertaking a key square received a free 1:10 000-scale map. These were not included with the main packs, but were dispatched direct from the main OS offices at Southampton – an action for which the GA staff in Sheffield were duly grateful!

Naturally, the packs had to be prepared in advance, and it felt like a considerable gesture of faith when we signed the order for 1,500 of them. Even without the maps, they were surprisingly bulky, and seemed to be filling up every bit of spare corridor space at GA Headquarters before the survey got fully under way.

Organisation at Headquarters

As we soon began to realise, the logistics of the Land Use – UK project were a mammoth task. Julia Legg held the organisation and prioritisation of activity together with a wonderfully cool demeanour, and we had lined up some volunteer help in the allocation of squares. Even so, it soon became apparent that supplementary staff were needed to help administer the project. Jonathan Taffs and, later, Sara Smith joined us and were to prove invaluable and enthusiastic helpers at Sheffield for a period of about four months.

Jonathan and Sara could not have been employed without the financial help that arrived in the nick of time from two charitable trusts which had been impressed by the idea of Land Use – UK. Originally, we had hoped for substantial commercial support, and had good reason to expect it. However, it did not materialise, and the Dennis Curry Charitable Trust and the Ernest Cook Trust between them came to the rescue and contributed considerable sums to keep the project afloat.

Allocating the squares

A week or two after the launch, a trickle of recruitment forms appeared in the post at the Sheffield HQ. The trickle became a steady stream, turning to a flood by the beginning of March. In helping to handle the volume, the volunteer work of Ralph and Marie Hebden, working as 'square allocators', was crucial.

Ralph and Marie had recently retired from teaching posts in school and university respectively, having served both the GA and geography in general throughout their working lives. They responded to our call for volunteers to help in allocating areas to schools which registered, and we can but wonder if they knew what they were letting themselves in for …

As registrations were received, the fee was checked by the HQ staff and the forms passed to Ralph and Marie, who had been installed in the GA's editorial office. As well as their desk, there was an expanse of wall upon which they posted two large Ordnance Survey maps which covered the entire United Kingdom. The available squares were marked on the maps with blue dots. These steadily changed to a rash of red (allocated urban) and green (allocated rural) as the days passed.

Operating with the precision of military strategists, Ralph and Marie checked each grid reference provided by the registering school and then sought to allocate the nearest available key square. The forms included the question of how far the school was prepared to let its team travel to its survey square, and the allocation process had to take this into account. Expressed like this, the operation sounds easy, but in practice that was often far from the case. The process depended upon first being able to locate the school accurately: most of them were adept at quoting their postcode, but far fewer were able to provide their own OS grid reference, either accurately or at all. Consequently, detective work with road atlases and town plans was frequently needed before allocation could begin.

Local squares

Where a key square could not be found within a school's range, a 'local square' was offered instead. These were not part of the stratified sample, but provided material supplementary to the central survey. They also turned out to be an invaluable source of data for local initiatives and for other checking processes.

'We were surprised to find that we could hear the wind rustling through the crops …'

Photo: Tony Dodsworth

Twinning

This was a system by which schools in contrasting areas which wished to share data and experiences of Land Use – UK could be 'twinned'. It was a parallel operation to the allocation of squares, and was mounted by Mo Morron and Pat Partington during their visits to GA Headquarters, helped by Diane Wright and other members of the GA staff. The twinning system is described in some detail in Chapter 10.

The initial response

Interest in the project came from all over the country. Junior and even infant schools were as keen as secondary schools and sixth-form colleges. Retired teachers offered their services, including some who had been out in the 1960s as part of Alice Coleman's survey and fancied the task again. However, the response from universities was disappointing, despite the distribution of information to all the delegates at the RGS-IGB annual conference at Strathclyde. This outlined how institutions of higher education could help, but in the end only a few university departments involved their undergraduate students in the survey.

It was encouraging to find teachers from as far afield as the Channel Islands and even Europe phoning in to ask if they could be included in the project, even though the Ordnance Survey's gift of maps did not extend so far. In the event, the Channel Islands Planning Board and the Ordnance Survey of Northern Ireland both rose nobly to the occasion and provided comparable maps for the schools in their territories.

As the GA's Annual Conference approached in April 1996, it became time to take stock. About half the key squares in England and Wales had been taken up, but rather fewer in Scotland. This was not surprising, because about 200 of the squares lay in highland or border areas remote from schools and indeed from any form of human habitation. This level of take-up was moderately encouraging, but it was clear that some persuasion and pro-active recruitment might be needed to get the more remote squares covered.

More publicity

The next target for publicity was the Conference, held at Southampton University. There we would seek volunteers from the masses passing on their way to the lectures, seminars and publishers' exhibition. Extra interest was to be generated by a lecture during the main body of the conference and a 'Masterclass' conducted by Colin Barr, one of the devisors of the survey.

The National Steering Committee was given generous exhibition space in a prominent location, and a desk was staffed there throughout the Conference. This was very successful: there were almost always knots formed by enthusiastic recruits stopping by to talk about the project and in turn cajoling their colleagues to volunteer themselves or their schools. Some teachers would gaze silently at the array of dots on the map for several minutes before offering to join in, while others would bounce up with scarcely a second thought and offer to take on two or three more squares. The enthusiasm of the staff at the stall spread infectiously, and we began to sense the first intimation of likely success.

At the last minute Colin Barr was prevented from attending to lead the Masterclass, but Caroline Hallam, one of his colleagues from the Merlewood ITE Research Station, deputised with aplomb. After explaining to a group of potential leaders how the survey would work in practice, she led a large coach-load out to Southampton's rain-swept rural fringes for the first major field-training session of the project. At the end of the morning the group returned, fairly well soaked, but full of enthusiasm for returning to the roots of geography. As one Head of Department remarked, 'I don't seem to have been out with a map and looked over a gate into a field for years. I now remember what I liked about geography when I first studied it!'

The GA President, Mike Morrish, who was also Chair of the Land Use – UK National Steering Committee, alluded to this in his speech at the Annual Dinner on the last night of the Conference:

> *This morning, as I was walking through the entrance hall, I saw a group of bedraggled teachers wearing sodden anoraks returning from the Land Use – UK Masterclass. And do you know – they were smiling! They could only have been geographers ...*

Training and support

The Southampton Masterclass was the first of several similar events which were held up and down the country. Three days later a northern equivalent event was held at Liverpool Hope University, where an enthusiastic group organised a full-day conference which included a field trial.

In Hertfordshire the meeting was attended by a representative of the County Planning Department, who offered to help by providing maps for both local and key squares. In Brighton, the University Map Librarian made a similarly helpful offer. At all these meetings teachers welcomed the opportunity to discuss strategies for the survey with each other as well as getting clarification about such matters as survey categories and ways of presenting the results.

The helpline

For those who could not get to a meeting, we established a helpline system. This operated from GA Headquarters, where the problem was either fielded or passed out to the 'duty' member of the National Steering Committee. I did three weeks as the member on call, and was fascinated by the range of queries that came through. Sometimes the callers only required confirmation that they had worked out the correct solutions to the problems; others just wanted to talk about how to organise the surveys. There were very few questions about how to apply the categories or distinguish between them, even though the Committee had been conscious when selecting them that it was necessary to steer a middle line between absolute precision and practicability. This was particularly the case with the urban categories, where it had been tempting to have a much more complex set. However, we knew that this may well have led to greater error in the end, particularly as much of the work would be done by groups with little experience of urban survey practice.

My most anxious moment as a helpline 'Samaritan' came when I was told that there was a caller from Londonderry on the line with a 'problem'. My mind immediately equated 'problem' with 'Troubles' and I visualised a class becoming unwittingly caught up in the civil disturbances of the Province. I was relieved to find that the problem was merely a question of which crayon to use for a marginal category! The teacher reported cheerfully that 'there was no trouble at all' in completing the key square in such an apparently strife-torn area.

We received some queries by letter. One of these threw an interesting light on the changing nature of our increasingly multicultural society. The survey team from a Bradford school, situated in a mainly Muslim area, enquired why it seemed that only Christian churches were marked on the maps. Was this discrimination? I hastened to refer this to the OS, and was informed by one of their Education Officers that in the legends on newer maps the expression 'church with spire' is replaced by 'place of worship with spire, minaret or dome'.

Mailings

Following the distribution of the Packs, the survey groups (mainly schools, but there was a sprinkling of other organisations taking part) had to return a confirmation form which was the cue for their OS maps to be sent to them. But it didn't end there: in

Ministerial visit

Perhaps the most high-profile event of the survey was the visit one morning in June of the Under-Secretary of State for the Environment, James Clappison MP, to Sunny Bank Junior School in Potters Bar, Hertfordshire — see photo. The Minister went out with the 8- and 9-year-old surveyors and their Headteacher, Keith Hooper, who had led the survey work in the school. The pupils proved eloquent and persuasive guardians of their local environment, and in the bright summer sunshine the Minister listened attentively for almost an hour as they explained their views about preserving open local space and keeping paths free from dog-fouling.

As the class and the Minister trudged single-file across a field of setaside farmland with the M25 significantly in view, a golden photo-opportunity was provided. Next day *The Independent* carried a photofeature with a shot of the scene and a caption about the survey. The intriguing, if not wholly accurate, headline read: 'Eyes down, single-file please, for the biggest geography lesson in the world'.

May, June, September and October they received further mailings of survey news and material. Two of these contained detailed advice on media contact, complete with guidelines and suggested formats, and they proved particularly fruitful. The firm Communications Management monitored the survey for the GA and expressed surprise at the amount of local publicity generated by schools which had followed the advice zealously. More than fifty schools achieved radio or TV coverage — sometimes both — and the press reports and photo-features ran into hundreds, as the GA's thick book of press cuttings graphically reveals.

Filling in the blanks

As late as June, with the survey fully under way, we were still concerned about some areas where the full share of key squares had not been taken up. Although nearly 1,400 schools were registered by this stage, about two-fifths of them were engaged on local squares only. This had the makings of a problem, as the survey would not be valid if there were significant gaps in the carefully calculated stratified sample.

Erica Downie, President of the Scottish Association of Geography Teachers, took us a big step towards resolving the problem. She had been at the Southampton Conference and promised to do all she could to improve the Scottish take-up. She was as good as her word, writing personally to many schools in outlying areas to persuade them to undertake the survey of remote squares. Soon there were encouraging colour changes among the Scottish dots on the master map. Even so, as the summer term progressed, a quarter of the key squares remained unclaimed.

For a short time the total went into reverse when a number of schools backed out of their commitments for a variety of reasons: illness, other business, or simple lack of organisation. This was very discouraging and frustrating for the organisers, particularly as it became clear that some of these squares could have been allocated elsewhere if the intention not to participate had been signalled earlier. However, it was clear that many of the schools had had every intention of doing the survey, but had allowed themselves to be caught unawares by the pressures which inevitably build up towards the end of the academic year. In some cases teachers gallantly undertook the entire task of surveying in their spare time when plans for school parties to do it had failed.

The Geographical Task Force

Fortunately, there remained another strategy to fall back on. The National Steering Committee had foreseen that there might be unclaimed squares, and had proposed a Geographical Task Force to complete the survey during the summer vacation.

Photo: Peter Hoare

Volunteers for the Force were sought from the Royal Geographical Society and the Royal Scottish Geographical Society, as well as from the GA, SAGT and AGTW. This resulted in a small but growing register of potential helpers being compiled during spring and early summer.

We were greatly heartened when Russell Chapman, from University College School, Hampstead, agreed to take on the organisation of the Force. After many years of organising the GA's Annual Conferences, his persuasive efforts were now directed towards the Task Force volunteers. He induced many to undertake marathon journeys to out-of-the-way places so that another key square could be ticked off, and even pulled off the occasional coup by persuading certain volunteers to take on mass allocations. The Highland raid detailed in Chapter 11 is the result of one of these.

The Geographical Task Force had a limited amount of financial support available to help students and other volunteers with the cost of surveying remote squares.

By the time recruiting ceased in mid-August, almost 200 of the previously unclaimed squares had been allocated to the Task Force. The volunteers turned out to be very prompt in submitting reliable, well-observed surveys. In the end, when the time came to draw the line and begin to calculate the preliminary results, the combined effort of schools, teachers, groups and the Task Force had produced surveys of more than 90% of the 1029 key squares. We could be confident that the results would be significant.

James Clappison, MP, Under-Secretary of State for the Environment, joins the survey team from Sunny Bank Junior School, Potters Bar

Some of the practical problems from the field

Colours

The need to establish uniformity of colour on the completed maps was an early priority of the Survey Design group. A deal was completed with Crayola, the coloured-pencil makers, to supply sets of 24 pencils at a discount rate. These were included with the instruction packs sent to the schools. The fanciful names of some of the colours, such as Wild Watermelon and Atomic Tangerine, caused smiles. However, Atomic Tangerine came to the rescue once the survey was under way, when it was quickly realised that using the original choices of black and grey to show residential and commercial premises respectively was not satisfactory. They were too similar to produce distinctive or attractive maps. A supplementary order went out in the second mailing for Atomic Tangerine to replace grey and thus introduce the necessary contrast.

Transport confusion

The survey designers believed that the designation 'transport' should be given only to through routes and that streets such as cul-de-sacs and crescents that only provide access within housing estates should count as part of the residential land use.

Although there was a conceptual logic to this, the fact that only some 'roads' were to be classified as 'transport' caused the greatest puzzlement among the young surveyors. A similar perplexity arose about the decision to include allotments as part of residential use, on the basis that they represented domestic curtilage rather than a separate land use.

The vertical dimension

As in many other surveys, the problem of how to record the variety of land uses which can occur in the vertical dimension remained unsolved. In rural areas this rarely mattered, but elsewhere there was concern about the need always to record ground-floor use, rather than the dominant use of a building. In the case of shops surmounted by twenty-storey office blocks, such concern was well-founded. No satisfactory solution could be found that could be turned into a general survey instruction.

Remote locations and other problems

Some key squares were so remote that there was some difficulty with initial allocation, particularly in the Highlands. Members of the Geographical Task Force covered many of the more isolated and wild areas.

A frequent and understandable complaint from schools was that their rural key square was so uniform in its content that it represented little challenge to their surveying talents. This was also a problem in coastal areas, where many squares from the 'coastal landscape' class had large amounts of sea in them.

Only one case was reported of a school being refused access to survey a square. This was in Northumberland, and the manager of the large estate concerned gave the danger from logging operations as the reason. Everywhere else managers of estates, factories, public institutions and commercial complexes, as well as numerous farmers and landowners, seem to have been supportive, helpful, and often enthusiastic in providing information to the groups which they welcomed onto their property.

Grid-reference confusion

Land Use – UK's reference to the squares depended on the Ordnance Survey national grid-reference system. Some schools were confused by this, although they could work on the old letter-and-number system associated with the 1:25 000-scale maps. Others professed no knowledge of the system at all. A briefing paper on reading the

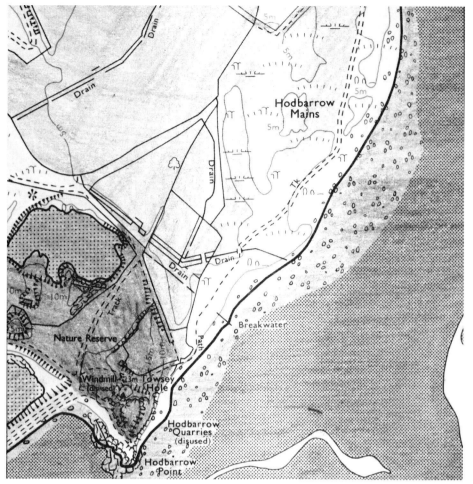

*A coastal square
Based upon the Ordnance
Survey map with the
permission of the
Controller of Her
Majesty's Stationery
Office © Crown copyright*

references was provided by the OS and supplied, along with supplementary guidance, in the instruction packs.

In spite of this a succession of teachers rang the helpline for step-by-step guidance from very first principles. From this the suspicion arose that not only did some schools not teach simple map-referencing, but also that there were no OS maps of any kind among their geography resources. Hopefully, Land Use – UK will have gone some way to repairing this omission.

Grid decisions

The desire to calculate the percentages of land uses in each square as well as just mapping them led to the need to provide a sampling mechanism. The idea of simply dividing each kilometre square into a hundred smaller squares via a 10 x 10 grid was considered and rejected, because if the dominant land use in each small square was recorded, there was a good chance that some small minority uses would always be missed.

The expert advice was that 'stratified point sampling' was necessary to record efficiently. In this, a 10 x 10 grid is still used, but this time to produce a hundred points of intersection, and it is these points that are recorded. The sampling experts advised that the points should not include any right at the edges of the square, so a double grid, with one slightly offset on the other, had to be used. The survey designers were worried that this concept might defeat the inexperienced, but the schools rallied to the challenge and few problems or questions about the grid were reported.

Chapter 4:
Generating the results

Rex Walford

All the survey teams were asked to return the results of their work to GA headquarters at Sheffield. There the completed maps and forms were registered and checked against the original database.

Parcels of forms were sent from Sheffield at regular intervals to the Land Use – UK Results Office, which was established at the Institute of Terrestrial Ecology at Monks Wood near Huntingdon. The ITE loaned an office, computers and other equipment, and from 8 July 1996 two student recruits, Avril Lawrence and Katy George, who became key helpers in the project. Under the guidance of David Cooper, the Results Team Leader, and ITE staff members, they began the considerable task of setting up a computer database for the results of Tasks 1 and 2.

The trickle of returns became a torrent by the end of July, and all through August the task of cataloguing the mass of data and checking the location of the returns continued.

Checking Tasks 1 and 2

The 100 points recorded on the maps through the point-sampling method for each square were put into the database, and at the same time the percentages of land use calculated by the schools were checked – and in some cases put right! With a total of nearly 2,000 key and local squares surveyed, it is a sobering thought that some 200,000 pieces of basic land-use information are now stored on the database. The initial analysis of percentage totals is only a tiny fraction of the work which can be undertaken.

Checking Task 3

Task 3 asked for views and visions of future change, and after taking expert advice from Cambridge University experts in qualitative analysis, a series of broad categories had been devised for each of the questions. The format of the questions had been deliberately planned to prompt open-ended responses, but naturally this increased the complexity of the analysis. To cope with this, a team of teachers conducted a one-day pilot exercise at Monks Wood before full processing started. They worked through a hundred forms to see if the categorisation was satisfactory. As a result of the exercise some adjustments to the categories were made and a Task 3 Results Team was set up, with teacher volunteers at the core. Their work was done in a separate office, working carefully but steadily through each of the 'views and visions' response sheets.

Many schools had completed the Task 3 sheets in considerable detail, and the forms caused much discussion as well as needing sensitive interpretation. Though half-a-dozen experienced teachers gave up part of their summer holiday to help code the results, it was only possible to work through those of the key squares in the time available before the preliminary results leaflet had to be prepared. The local squares would have to wait.

Once a fair number of results had been received, Colin Barr and Philip Kivell visited the Results Office to consult with the recording team. Colin, based at the ITE Merlewood Research Station in Grange-over-Sands, and Philip, from the University of Keele, are experts on rural and urban data respectively. The discussions revolved around what kinds of summation of data and analysis would be necessary as the conclusion of the receiving period approached.

Deadlines

It was hoped that all the results would be received by 31 August, but inevitably some teachers and Task Force members were delayed either in surveying or in sending on the results. Effective 'chasing' work went on from GA Headquarters; most late returns had honest hard-luck stories attached to them, and it was only very rarely that a school reported shamefacedly that not only had it failed to do its survey but it had also failed to let the GA know about its change of mind. These isolated incidents caused much gnashing of teeth in the project committee, since there was no doubt that most of the missed squares could have been reallocated easily if only the withdrawal of intention to survey had been notified in time.

Though earlier surveys had taken several years to survey and report, and had then given themselves no particular deadlines for presenting results, the National Steering Committee of Land Use – UK imposed upon itself the task of completing the work in the summer of 1996 and having preliminary results available in time for schools to use in the proposed Geography Action Week in mid-November. The task was tightened further by the subsequent decision to organise a launch of the results at a conference at the Royal Geographical Society on Monday 4 November 1996.

Thus a cut-off point for the inclusion of returns in the preliminary results leaflet had to be made so that analysis could begin, and in order to allow at least a minimal time for printing and distribution to all participating schools. The cut-off point was also influenced by the fact that student helpers who helped Land Use – UK as a holiday job had to be back at their universities by early October, and that teacher volunteers helping with the Task 3 returns had an even earlier deadline.

So by late September, the results were being scrutinised anxiously to ensure that there were sufficient returns in the national and regional sub-divisions, and that all the ITE landscape and proposed urban townscape classes were effectively represented.

The power of the Countryside Information System and similar computer programs to analyse the data made the eventual compilation of figures much less arduous than it would have been in the 1930s or 1960s. Colin Barr, Robin Fuller and Philip Kivell spared time from their own schedules to work on the analysis and interpretation of data of Tasks 1 and 2, while Rex Walford handled the final analysis of the Task 3 forms.

By the time the last student helper, Tonny Olesen (working for his PhD while at ITE and awaiting some results on his own research), closed the Results Office at the end of October, the main data on the key squares had been processed and made available for the preliminary results leaflet. Much of the data from the local squares remains to be analysed and is a rich untapped source of material. Further funding now obtained from trusts and research bodies will enable this valuable data to be exploited to the full in future years.

At the launch of the results Colin Barr, Robin Fuller, Philip Kivell and Rex Walford (deputising for David Cooper) made presentations about the results. A brief overview follows in Chapter 5, with more detailed analysis and commentary in Chapters 6 and 7.

Photo: Peter Hoare

Ashley Kent, Rex Walford and Mike Morrish discussing the preliminary results of the survey

Chapter 5:
The overall picture

Rex Walford

In the short time available before the preliminary results were published, it was possible to record and analyse the results from some 800 key squares. Some of the major findings are summarised in the panel:

- Over 10% of the land of the UK is built-up.
- A third of England is covered by arable land, but the proportion of arable land in the remainder of the UK is less than one-tenth.
- Land devoted to agricultural use (arable and grassland) makes up well over half (55%) of Britain.
- Almost half the land in built-up areas is residential, followed by transport uses.
- Only 3.6% of land in the urban areas of Britain is now in industrial use; the largest regional proportion (8.6%) is in the West Midlands.
- The percentage of open space (9.6%) in urban areas is nearly three times that devoted to industry.
- The area of forest and woodland (12%) in Britain in 1996 is double the area recorded in the 1930s.
- Pylons or communications towers were identified as landscape features in 25% of the areas surveyed.

The tables and diagrams in this chapter show the combined results of the rural and urban surveys and comparisons with past surveys. Much fuller results accompanied by detailed commentaries appear in Chapters 6 and 7.

It is important that the surveyors and data-users understand the output from the sample-based approach. The field-survey data are used to calculate the average contents of each ITE Land Class. As the samples are placed at random, this average is then said to represent the whole of that class throughout its British 'range' (i.e. the extent of land covered by that particular class). By reference to this range, which we know exactly from the ITE survey data, and by estimating the average land use from field data, we can build up a picture of land use and derive estimates for each ITE Land Class. We can aggregate the class totals to give results for all of Britain, and we can look at regions within Britain based on their class composition.

The information given here includes:
1. Data for land use in the UK, including both urban and rural squares.
2. Data for land use in England, including both urban and rural squares. This also illustrates broad differences of land use in English regions.
3. A comparison of the percentage of some categories of land use for Britain recorded by the First LUS (1930s) and Land Use – UK. Note that data for Northern Ireland were not gathered in the First LUS.
4. A comparison of the percentage of some categories of land use for England and Wales recorded by the First LUS (1930s), Second LUS (1960s) and Land Use – UK.
5. A comparison of the percentage of some categories of land use for Britain recorded by the DofE Countryside Survey of 1990 (organised by ITE) and Land Use – UK.

6 A comparison of the percentage of some categories of land use for Britain recorded by Ministry of Agriculture estimates for 1995 and Land Use – UK.

7 Tables to show the presence of particular 'national issue' features in rural and urban key squares.

In relation to 3, 4, 5 and 6, it should be noted that although the categories recorded were essentially similar in each of the surveys, marginal differences of categorisation and interpretation may be responsible for some of the differences.

1 Land use in the UK

The amount of built-up land (including residential, commercial and industrial) found by the survey corresponds closely with that estimated by other methods. Note the considerable differences between the four parts of the UK. The figures for Northern Ireland are based on a relatively small number of squares.

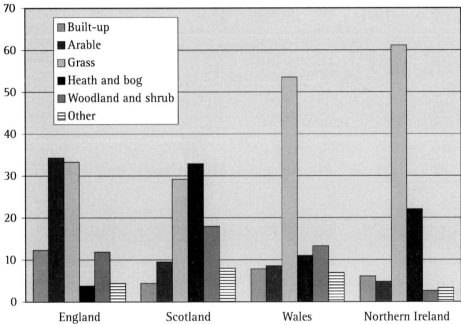

Description	England	Scotland	Wales	NI	UK
Built-up	12.3	4.4	7.8	6.1	10.3
Arable	34.3	9.5	8.5	4.8	22.0
Grass	33.3	29.2	53.5	61.1	34.2
Heath and bog	3.8	32.9	11.0	22.1	14.8
Woodland and shrub	11.9	18.0	13.3	2.6	13.1
Rocks and quarries	0.6	2.8	1.5	0.1	1.4
Wetland and water	1.4	2.4	1.3	1.3	1.7
Other	2.4	2.8	4.1	1.9	2.5

Figure 5.1 Percentage land-use figures in the UK (1996), based on preliminary data from 800 of the rural and urban key squares

2 Land use in England

The regions are identified more precisely in Chapter 2 (Figure 2.3). Amounts of built-up land vary notably in the regions: in the North-West and South-East it is double that recorded in the North.

East Anglia, traditionally 'the bread-basket of England', is still pre-eminent in the proportion of arable land, which is three times that of the North-West. East Anglia has the lowest percentage of grassland, while the highest is in the West. The North has the most forest, followed closely by the South-West

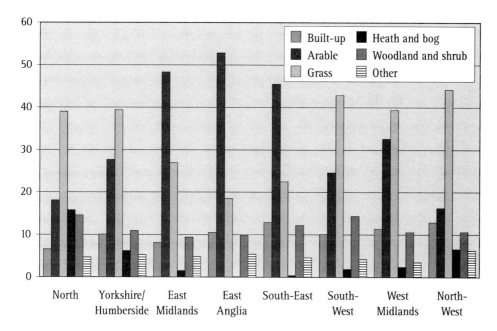

Description	North	Yorkshire/ Humberside	East Midlands	East Anglia	South- East	South- West	West Midlands	North- West
Built-up	6.6	10.1	8.1	10.5	12.9	10.1	11.4	12.9
Arable	18.1	27.7	48.3	52.8	45.5	24.6	32.6	16.3
Grass	39.0	39.4	27.0	18.5	22.5	42.9	39.4	44.2
Heath and bog	15.8	6.2	1.5	0.1	0.4	1.9	2.4	6.6
Woodland and shrub	14.6	10.9	9.4	9.8	12.2	14.4	10.6	10.6
Rocks and quarries	1.2	1.1	0.4	0.1	0.3	0.3	0.4	1.2
Wetland and water	1.5	1.5	2.5	1.9	0.9	1.0	0.8	1.8
Other	2.0	2.7	1.9	3.4	3.4	2.9	2.3	3.3

Figure 5.2
Percentage land-use figures in the English regions (1996), based on preliminary data from 800 of the rural and urban key squares

3 Comparison of the First LUS (1930s) with Land Use – UK (1996)

Commentary

Comparisons of Land Use – UK survey data with the data from previous surveys must be treated with caution, since the conditions and instructions of survey and the quality of the surveying may vary. However, the categorisation of arable land, combined grassland and woodland across the three surveys bears broad comparison.

It is notable that, although the amount of arable land in Britain has changed little from the 1930s to the 1990s, the amount of forest and woodland appears to have more than doubled. The activity of the Forestry Commission in creating new plantation areas is likely to account for a substantial part of this.

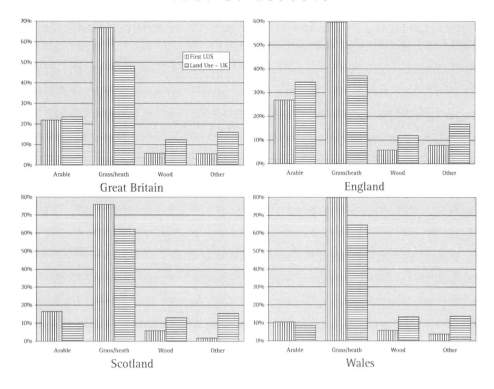

Great Britain

England

Scotland

Wales

First LUS (1930s) (total coverage)			Land Use – UK (1996) (rural squares sample)		
A. Great Britain					
Arable		21.4%			22.2%
Orchards, etc.		0.5%			0.4%
Permanent grass	33.5%	**66.8%**	Grass	32.4%	**46.3%**
Rough grazing	33.3%		Heath and bog	13.9%	
Forest and woodland		5.7%			11.9%
B. England					
Arable and horticulture		26.8%			34.3%
Permanent grass	47.7%	**59.6%**	Grass	33.3%	**37.1%**
Rough grazing	11.9%		Heath and bog	3.8%	
Forest and woodland		5.7%			11.9%
C. Scotland					
Arable and horticulture		16.5%			9.5%
Permanent grass	7.7%	**75.9%**	Grass	29.2%	**62.1%**
Rough grazing	68.2%		Heath and bog	32.9%	
Forest and woodland		5.8%			13.0%
D. Wales					
Arable and horticulture		10.5%			8.5%
Permanent grass	42.5%	**79.9%**	Grass	53.5%	**64.5%**
Rough grazing	37.4%		Heath and bog	11.0%	
Forest and woodland		5.8%			13.3%

Figure 5.3
Comparison of the First
LUS (1930s) with Land
Use – UK (1996)

Sources
Summary tables of First
LUS in Stamp (1948),
3rd edition 1962, page
196 Tables in
Chapter 6.

4 Comparison of data for England and Wales from the three land-use surveys

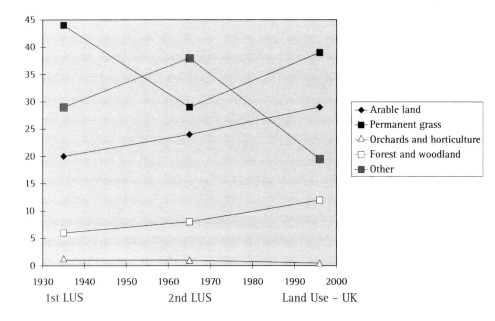

1st LUS   2nd LUS   Land Use – UK

Legend:
- ◆ Arable land
- ■ Permanent grass
- △ Orchards and horticulture
- □ Forest and woodland
- ■ Other

Figure 5.4
Comparison of data for England and Wales from the three land-use surveys

	First LUS (1930s)	Second LUS (1960s)	Land Use – UK (1996)
Arable land	19.7%	24.4%	30.0%
Permanent grass	44.1%	29.2%	35.3%
Orchards and horticulture	0.9%	0.9%	0.6%
Forest and woodland	5.7%	8.0%	11.9%

Sources
Summary tables of First LUS in Stamp (1948), 3rd edition 1962, page 196
Table of Second LUS figures in Coleman (1977), page 100
Tables in Chapter 6.

Commentary

The figures show that the amount of arable land in England and Wales has steadily increased since the Depression years. Permanent grassland was at a low point in the 1960s but has since recovered – possibly due to reclamation in hilly marginal areas. The steady increase in woodland in England and Wales matches the figures for Britain (Figure 5.3).

5 A comparison of the percentage of some categories of land use for Britain recorded by the DofE Countryside Survey of 1990 (organised by ITE) and Land Use – UK

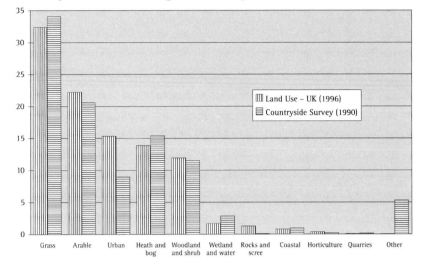

Figure 5.5

A comparison of the percentage of some categories of land use for Britain recorded by the DofE Countryside Survey of 1990 (organised by ITE) and Land Use – UK

6 A comparison of the percentage of some categories of land use for Britain recorded by Ministry of Agriculture estimates for 1995 and Land Use – UK

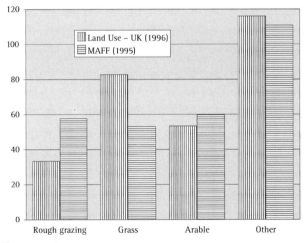

Figure 5.6

A comparison of the percentage of some categories of land use for Britain recorded by Ministry of Agriculture estimates for 1995 and Land Use – UK

Commentary

Figures 5.5 and 5.6 compare Land Use – UK with the ITE's 1990 Countryside Survey and the 1995 estimates of the Ministry of Agriculture, Forestry and Fisheries (MAFF). The ITE survey used satellite images backed up by a sample-based field survey.

In the major agricultural categories there is general agreement between these two sets of figures and those of Land Use – UK.

Land Use – UK records a slightly larger proportion of arable land and a slightly smaller proportion of grassland than ITE, but the differences are not significant. Land Use – UK included a set of specifically urban squares in its sample, which partially explains the higher proportion of urban land recorded.

The total area of agricultural land estimated by MAFF and recorded by Land Use – UK is remarkably similar.

7 Tables to show the presence of particular Task 2 ('national issue') features in rural and urban key squares

	New housing	Supermarkets	Corner shops	Pylons	Setaside
England	14.5	1.4	11.4	26.2	35.1
Scotland	5.7	0.1	3.6	15.1	12.3
Wales	7.3	1.1	5.4	15.6	15.7
Northern Ireland	11.0	7.4	31.4	18.2	0.0

Figure 5.7
Task 2 features
(rural key squares)

	New housing	Supermarkets	Corner shops	Pylons	Setaside
England	76.5	24.6	72.2	24.7	0.0
Scotland	54.5	36.4	66.7	18.2	0.0
Wales	100.0	25.0	91.7	25.0	0.0
Northern Ireland	63.0	28.0	76.5	23.8	0.0

Figure 5.8
Task 2 features
(urban key squares)

Source: Preliminary data from 800 of the rural and urban key squares, Land Use – UK 1996. The figures for Northern Ireland are based on a relatively small number of squares.

For details of the 'national issues' see Chapter 1 and the relevant sections of Chapters 6 and 7.

Views and visions

Here are a few brief general conclusions from the preliminary analysis, to give a flavour of the responses to Land Use – UK's Task 3. See Chapter 8 for detailed commentary.

- Traffic and its related pollution are singled out as being the major cause of environmental concern.
- The UK of the future is pictured as a place where land is increasingly swallowed up by urban development.
- Most school pupils who surveyed urban areas want to see better housing and quieter roads. In rural areas of the UK there is a desire to see no great change, but there is a wish for better access to the countryside.
- More people, more noise, more pollution is generally expected in twenty years time. Everyone is expected to own a car, with the roads being 'total chaos'.
- Pupils were attracted by the character of the rural areas they surveyed. They were largely described in positive terms such as 'peaceful', beautiful', 'unspoilt'. In contrast 'depressing' and 'run-down' were descriptions frequently applied to the urban areas.

Discussions and conclusions

The Land Use - UK sample-based field survey was able to generate the most detailed survey of the land of Great Britain for over 30 years. When Sir Dudley Stamp in the 1930s, and Dr Alice Coleman in the 1960s, recorded the landscape of Great Britain, the logical choice was and 'inventory' to record the land in its entirety. Stamp's survey required 20,000 'voluntary surveyors', and 250,000 schoolchildren. His results took 15 years to bring together and summarise in his excellent book *The Land of Britain: its use and misuse* (Stamp 1948.)

Sampling cannot claim to produce a survey as complete as Stamp's or Coleman's, but it has allowed us to generate statistics quickly, efficiently and effectively. Schoolchildren have been able to experience the procedures of a land use survey. Perhaps most importantly, it has adopted the sort of techniques which are used by professionals in science, business and industry the world over - the use of a representative statistical sample to minimise the recording effort, while maximising the information. This lesson is very worthwhile, whether learned in geography or in any other subject area.

Chapter 6: A commentary on the rural results

Colin Barr and Robin Fuller

The maps and statistics in this account are based on 404 of the 500 rural key squares. Although the sample is representative of the ITE Land Classes and perfectly acceptable for estimating national land cover, some classes were under-represented and this caused larger standard errors than is desirable.

The following sections present:

- land-use data for all Great Britain
- sample output maps for Great Britain
- summary statistics for England, Scotland and Wales
- further subdivisions based upon landscapes and administrative regions.

Description	Total area (km²)	Mean (% of GB)	Std error (% of GB)
Urban squares	*6,320*	*2.6*	-
1 Arable land	53,380	22.2	1.1
2 Horticulture, orchards, vineyards and soft fruit	856	0.4	0.1
3 Grass	77,840	32.4	1.4
4 Heathland and bog	33,320	13.9	1.3
5 Woodland and shrub	28,670	11.9	0.9
6 Inland rocks and scree	3,078	1.3	0.2
7 Wetland and water	3,997	1.7	0.3
8 Coastal features	1,914	0.8	0.4
9 Quarries and other extractive industries	185	0.1	0.0
10 Agricultural buildings	1,032	0.4	0.0
11 Transport routes and features	5,882	2.4	0.2
12 Residential	8,079	3.4	0.4
13 Commercial and business uses	950	0.4	0.1
14 Industrial premises and utilities	689	0.3	0.1
15 Public institutions	1,705	0.7	0.2
16 Tended open space	2,511	1.0	0.2
17 Waste land and derelict buildings	792	0.3	0.1
18 Land in transition	370	0.2	0.0
19 Unsurveyed and 20 sea	8,651	3.6	0.0
Total	240,221	100.0	

Figure 7.1

The land use of Great Britain estimated from the Land Use – UK sample-based field surveys

Photo: Paula Richardson

Data for Great Britain

In Figure 6.1 the percentage land area for the urban squares is included for completeness.

The rural land cover of Britain is made up of four main types. Most important is **grassland,** which covers 32%. **Arable land** comes second with 22% of the total. These agricultural uses make up 55% of all Britain.

Heath and bog cover 14% of Britain's landscape, with **woodland** at 12%. Wetland **and water** make up nearly 2%, **rocks and scree** cover about 1% and **coastal habitats** a further 1%, showing that about 30% of Britain is semi-natural in character.

Built-up land covers 8% of the rural landscape, with recreational **open space** at about 1%. This built-up total should be added to the 2.6% developed land of urban areas, indicating that about 10% of Britain is under bricks, concrete and tarmac. Note that the standard errors give an idea of how much variation there might be in these estimates: widespread features have small standard errors, but rarer land-use types

Figure 6.2 Arable land   *Figure 6.3 Heath and bog*

may carry errors in estimates which are much larger.

These national statistics hide a wide range of variations between the different parts of Great Britain. These are recorded in the following maps and data tables. Because the estimation of the rarer land-use types in smaller regions is of lesser reliability, the 19 classes of the survey are simplified to give just eight major land-cover classes. To further simplify these preliminary results, standard errors are also omitted: that does not mean that the statistics are without some level of uncertainty.

Figure 6.2 is a map showing the estimated density of arable land; Figure 6.3 shows the estimated density of heath and bog, and Figure 6.4 shows the estimated density of grass. The maps use a colour scale to show cover, from the minimum level (dark red) to the maximum (yellow). These maps have been constructed using the ITE Land Classes to define a zonation and the statistics for average cover to estimate the arable, heath or grass cover within each zone. Note the dominance of arable farming in southern and eastern Britain, the grass farming regions of the south and west, and the heath and bog areas of northern and western Britain.

Data for England, Scotland and Wales

England has the most intensively used rural landscape in Britain. Arable farmland covers just over one-third of the surface and grassland another third. Other studies suggest that most of the grassland is used for intensive grazing, at least in the lowlands. Woodland and scrub make up 12% of the landscape, with just 4% heath and bog. Built-up areas are estimated to occupy 10% of rural England, or 13% of England when urban squares are added.

In Scotland, arable farming occupies less than 10% of the landscape, and even the amount of grassland, at 29%, is less than that found in England. In contrast to England, heath and bog are the most extensive cover type, representing a third of all Scotland. Figure 6.7 shows how the moorlands of Scotland are so much more extensive than those elsewhere in Britain. Woodland cover is no more than in England, although much of it is likely to be coniferous. The rugged nature of the landscape is shown by the greater proportions of bare rock and scree, with the lakes and lochs of Scotland also evident in the cover statistics. Built-up areas cover just 4% of the rural Scottish landscape.

Wales is remarkable for the extent of grassland at 54%, as shown in Figure 6.6. Arable farming, at 9%, occupies an even smaller proportion of the land than in Scotland. In other cover types, such as heath and bog or the urban category, the character of the landscape is intermediate between that of England and Scotland.

Data for environmental regions

In ITE's analyses of the data, Britain has been divided into four broad environmental regions: arable lowland, pastural lowland, marginal upland, and upland. These are based upon an aggregation of the 32 ITE Land Classes. It is important to remember

Figure 6.4 Grass

Figure 6.5
The land cover of England estimated from the Land Use – UK survey

Description	%	km²
Built-up	10.3	13,552
Arable	34.3	44,987
Grass	33.3	43,650
Heath and bog	3.8	5,020
Woodland and shrub	11.9	15,630
Rocks and quarries	0.6	729
Wetland and water	1.4	1,833
Other	2.8	3,611

Figure 6.6
The land cover of Wales estimated from the Land Use – UK survey

Description	%	km²
Built-up	7.6	1,572
Arable	8.5	1,760
Grass	53.5	11,140
Heath and bog	11.0	2,286
Woodland and shrub	13.3	2,758
Rocks and quarries	1.5	305
Wetland and water	1.3	272
Other	1.5	313

Figure 6.7
The land cover of Scotland estimated from the Land Use – UK survey

Description	%	km²
Built-up	4.1	3,214
Arable	9.5	7,484
Grass	29.2	23,050
Heath and bog	32.9	26,020
Woodland and shrub	13.0	10,280
Rocks and quarries	2.8	2,229
Wetland and water	2.4	1,892
Other	2.2	1,769

that these regions were based upon maps of climate and land form, not on land use: the land-cover data are thus independent of the regionalisation scheme. The broad environmental regions have been used to derive land-cover statistics, which are shown in tabular and map form in Figures 6.8–6.11.

Figure 6.8
The land cover of arable lowland landscapes

Note that a reasonably large quantity of grass is associated with the arable land; heath and bog are very rare; built-up areas are estimated to be at their most extensive in this landscape.

Description	%	km²
Built-up	11.8	9,555
Arable	45.3	36,525
Grass	24.7	19,890
Heath and bog	0.6	452
Woodland and shrub	11.6	9,378
Rocks and quarries	0.3	213
Wetland and water	1.4	1,126
Others	3.0	2,410

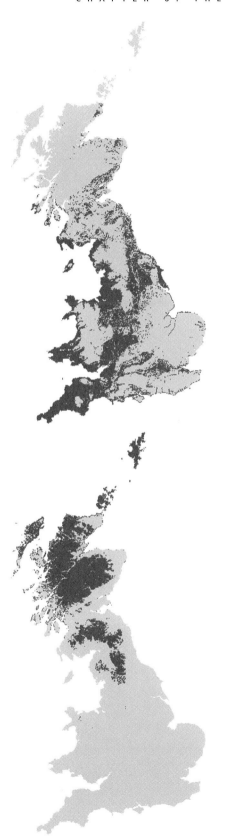

Description	%	km²
Built-up	10.1	6,794
Arable	25.4	17,155
Grass	44.2	29,790
Heath and bog	1.1	726
Woodland and shrub	11.8	7,960
Rocks and quarries	0.1	98
Wetland and water	1.1	742
Other	3.4	2,305

Figure 6.9
The land cover of pastural lowland landscapes

Note that grassland dominates, but that there is also a reasonably high quantity of arable land. Built-up areas are reasonably extensive.

Description	%	km²
Built-up	3.9	1,426
Arable	1.5	554
Grass	49.3	18,120
Heath and bog	24.3	8,942
Woodland and shrub	13.0	4,762
Rocks and quarries	3.6	1,340
Wetland and water	1.9	709
Other	0.6	208

Figure 6.10
The land cover of marginal upland landscapes

Note that grassland and heath are dominant, but that built-up areas are scarce. The extent of rock and quarries is far greater than in arable and pastural landscapes.

Figure 6.11
The land cover of upland landscapes

Note the dominance of the heath and bog class, followed by grass and woodland; there is very little built-up land. Upland landscapes are also characterised by the presence of bare rock and quarries.

Description	%	km²
Built-up	1.2	565
Arable	0.0	0
Grass	21.8	10,030
Heath and bog	50.4	23,200
Woodland and shrub	14.3	6,572
Rocks and quarries	3.5	1,612
Wetland and water	3.1	1,421
Other	1.7	770

Data for the English regions

As we have seen, the Department of the Environment also use a subdivision of England into eight regions (see Figure 2.3). Statistics for these regions follow (Figures 6.12–6.19).

Description	%	km²
Built-up	6.6	1020
Arable	18.1	2793
Grass	39.0	6024
Heath and bog	15.8	2437
Woodland and shrub	14.6	2257
Rocks and quarries	1.2	189
Wetland and water	1.5	231
Other	2.0	315

Figure 6.12
Northern Region

Description	%	km²
Built-up	10.1	1,554
Arable	27.7	4,268
Grass	39.4	6,072
Heath and bog	6.2	948
Woodland and shrub	10.9	1,675
Rocks and quarries	1.1	173
Wetland and water	1.5	235
Other	2.7	409

Figure 6.13
Yorkshire and
Humberside Region

Description	%	km²
Built-up	8.1	1,262
Arable	48.3	7,553
Grass	27.0	4,231
Heath and bog	1.5	235
Woodland and shrub	9.4	1,477
Rocks and quarries	0.4	61
Wetland and water	2.5	387
Other	1.9	292

Figure 6.14
East Midlands Region

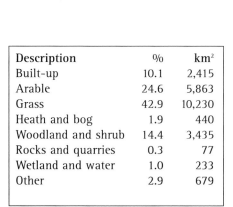

Description	%	km²
Built-up	10.5	1,328
Arable	52.8	6,652
Grass	18.5	2,327
Heath and bog	0.1	17
Woodland and shrub	9.8	1,237
Rocks and quarries	0.1	7
Wetland and water	1.9	244
Other	3.4	424

Figure 6.15
East Anglia Region

Description	%	km²
Built-up	12.9	3,506
Arable	45.5	12,368
Grass	22.5	6,111
Heath and bog	0.4	96
Woodland and shrub	12.2	3,312
Rocks and quarries	0.3	67
Wetland and water	0.9	254
Other	3.4	930

Figure 6.16
South-East Region

Description	%	km²
Built-up	10.1	2,415
Arable	24.6	5,863
Grass	42.9	10,230
Heath and bog	1.9	440
Woodland and shrub	14.4	3,435
Rocks and quarries	0.3	77
Wetland and water	1.0	233
Other	2.9	679

Figure 6.17
South-West Region

Figure 6.18
West Midlands Region

Description	%	km²
Built-up	11.4	1,488
Arable	32.6	4,240
Grass	39.4	5,130
Heath and bog	2.4	311
Woodland and shrub	10.6	1,376
Rocks and quarries	0.4	58
Wetland and water	0.8	105
Other	2.3	296

Figure 6.19
North-West Region

Description	%	km²
Built-up	12.9	947
Arable	16.3	1,199
Grass	44.2	3,247
Heath and bog	6.6	483
Woodland and shrub	10.6	777
Rocks and quarries	1.2	86
Wetland and water	1.8	132
Other	3.3	243

The regional statistics presented above reflect the findings of the analyses by landscape (Figures 6.8–6.11), with a trend from arable farming in the lowland east towards pastural land uses in the lowland west, with ever increasing amounts of heath and bog from south-east to north-west. Built-up areas are most extensive in lowland regions. Woodlands are remarkably uniform in distribution, though least extensive in the intensive arable regions of East Anglia and the East Midlands.

National issues

The survey of national issues gave interesting results (Figure 6.20). Setaside farmland was found in 25% of all squares. This does not necessarily mean that the setaside was extensive: it may have only covered the odd corner of a field in some of the squares. There is a much higher incidence of setaside in England, reflecting the much more intensive farming, hence greater potential for setaside.

New housing, the presence of corner shops, large supermarkets and pylons/communication towers were all much more prominent in England, with Wales usually in second place and Scotland third. This not only reflects the higher population densities in England but also the much greater extents of semi-natural land in Wales and Scotland.

Photo: Julia F Legg

Issue	Britain	England	Scotland	Wales
Setaside farmland	25.3	35.1	12.3	15.7
New housing (<5 years)	10.8	14.5	5.7	7.3
Corner shops	8.1	11.4	3.6	5.4
Large supermarkets	0.9	1.4	0	1.1
Pylons/communications towers	21.3	26.2	15.1	15.6

Figure 6.20 Percentage of one-kilometre squares where setaside farmland, new housing, corner shops, large supermarkets and pylons/communication towers were recorded in rural squares

Photo: Bryan Ledgard

The most frequently used
term to describe the
urban landscape was
'depressing'

Chapter 7: A commentary on the urban results

Philip Kivell

Introduction

Of the 500 urban key squares originally identified, 456 were taken up by teams of surveyors and 399 had usable results returned by the end of September 1996. This represents a response rate of 80% of the original total (and 88% of the squares that were actually taken up for survey). Given the complicated logistics of the exercise and the pressures on the time and resources of the surveyors, this was an excellent outcome. There was some variation in the response rate across the country, with regional returns ranging from 64% to 88%. The South-East, North-West and Scotland all achieved above-average returns. When analysed by settlement type, the largest numbers of squares, both allocated and returned, were in the 'mining and industrial' and 'urban' categories, but the best response rates came from 'Inner London' and from the 'prospering' and 'maturer' categories.

The overall pattern of urban land use

The percentage of land in each of the 20 categories was calculated for every urban square surveyed. The method is referred to in Chapter 3, but, briefly, it consisted of laying a 10 x 10 grid over each square and recording the category of land use at each of the 100 grid intersections. This gave a quick, simple and reasonably accurate measure of the amount of land in each category and further reinforced the appreciation of sampling techniques.

Before examining the results it is important to note that, especially in urban areas, the extent of a particular land use may not be a good guide to its importance in other terms. For example, transport is a large consumer of land but creates modest amounts of employment. However, offices often occupy small but intensively used sites and generate large numbers of jobs. It should also be remembered that surveyors only recorded ground-floor uses.

The results produced by this exercise are summarised in Figure 7.1. The figure indicates, reassuringly, that our sample of squares is truly urban in land-use character. If we exclude categories 1–10 (the 'countryside' uses), 16 (parks and playing fields), 19 (not surveyed) and 20 (sea), it can be seen that the urban group of squares is 80% covered by built-up land.

Figure 7.1
Summary of land use in
the urban squares

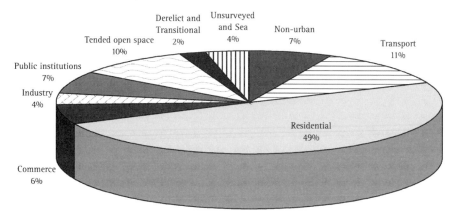

Residential housing

The largest single land use is the residential category (12) which, with 49.6% of the total (see Figure 7.2), is almost equal to all the other categories combined. This certainly matches the visual impression that one gets when travelling through British towns, or flying over them: houses, with their associated gardens, drives and service roads, are the dominant landscape feature. There is little comparable information available from elsewhere about the overall composition of urban land in Britain, but the figure for the residential category here is very close to the few estimates that have been published – for example that of Best (1981). Best's study was based upon data from 1961, so it would appear that the proportion of housing land in towns (although not the actual amount) has remained unchanged for 35 years. Another illustration of the dominance of residential land is shown by the fact that it covered more than half of the grid square in 326 out of the 399 squares surveyed.

Transport

The great importance of transport in today's urban society is illustrated by the fact that it is recorded as the second largest category of land use, accounting for almost one-eighth of the total. In two squares it was the majority land use. The category covers all forms of transport, so airports, sea ports, canals and railways are included, but the bulk clearly relates to road transport and associated features. It is worth noting that this category gave rise to some minor discrepancies in the survey concerning the recording of secondary roads within residential or industrial estates or large institutions. Most surveyors followed the rubric and recorded them under residential or industrial categories as appropriate, but a few put even the most minor roads in the transport category.

Open space

Perhaps surprisingly, tended open space, including parks, playgrounds and sport pitches, was the third most extensive land-use category. The proportion varied considerably across the sample: many squares had no tended open space, but one square in eight had more than 20 per cent of its land in this category. If there is a lingering image in Britain of densely built-up and industrialised towns, it is worth recording that this survey shows that there is as much tended open space in British towns as there is industrial and commercial land combined.

Industry and commerce

It has been well documented elsewhere that the relative economic and social importance of manufacturing industry has shrunk in recent years (see for example Champion and Townsend, 1990), but this survey shows that the importance of industry and utilities (category 14) is now very minor in land-use terms too. Overall this category accounted for just 3.6% of the total urban land surveyed, and from this point of view the description of the UK as an industrial country is no longer appropriate. Much more extensive, with 6% of the total, was the commercial category (13) which embraces offices, shops, hotels, warehouses and commercial entertainment facilities. Commercial activities often extend to upper-floor levels, so their true significance will be underestimated by this survey, which recorded ground-floor land uses only.

The regional pattern of urban land use

Much of the traditional pattern of regional distinctiveness in this country comes from the development of different economic activities. Therefore it might be expected that some of this pattern would be reflected in the results of Land Use – UK, but, as Figure 7.2 suggests, the regional variations are not particularly large.

The proportion of land in non-urban uses (categories 1–10) varied little from the overall average of 7%, except in the cases of East Anglia and Wales where it was 18.5 and 14.5% respectively. It would be plausible to suggest that this is because in both of these areas the towns are small and the countryside is never far away from the town centres. In fact it is also important to note that both regions have small numbers of sampled squares (only 7 in East Anglia) and this will affect their results in all categories.

If the four main categories of residential, transport, industry and commerce are taken together as the most urban of land uses, Figure 8.2 reveals that it is the towns of the East and West Midlands that are the most heavily built-up, with 77% and 78% respectively of their land in these four categories. The proportion of transport land varies little across the regions, but residential land does show substantial divergence, from minima of 34.3% in East Anglia and 38.5% in Scotland to a maximum of 61.1% in the East Midlands.

As far as industrial land is concerned, only Scotland, the North-West and the Midlands have percentages above the national urban average. In every region except the West Midlands, the amount of urban land given over to commerce and to public institutions exceeds that occupied by industry. This may provide a slim justification for the West Midlands' traditional description as the country's industrial heartland, but more broadly it is a pointer to the way in which Britain's cities now depend more upon the service sector than upon manufacturing.

Figure 7.2
Land-use categories by region (percentages)

Category of land use	Non-urban	Transport	Residential	Commerce	Industry	Public institutions	Tended open space	Derelict	Transitional	Unsurveyed and Sea
Category nos.	1–10	11	12	13	14	15	16	17	18	19–20
North	5.5	12.6	53.8	2.6	2.4	8.2	13.3	1.3	0.3	0
Yorkshire and Humberside	9.4	12.2	49.1	6.5	2.4	7.0	10.4	2.0	1.1	0
East Midlands	7.7	10.0	61.1	3.2	2.5	6.9	8.1	0.3	0.2	0
East Anglia	18.5	10.3	34.3	10.7	1.6	16.4	5.0	2.0	0.3	1.0
South-East	6.1	10.5	53.0	6.2	1.8	6.4	9.6	1.1	0.6	4.8
South-West	7.9	9.5	48.3	7.3	3.0	8.1	10.1	1.4	0.5	4.0
West Midlands	7.1	12.6	52.0	4.9	8.6	5.1	7.9	1.3	0.6	0
North-West	5.9	13.6	45.5	6.2	6.0	7.3	10.4	2.8	0.5	1.8
Wales	14.5	14.3	41.4	8.3	3.3	5.3	7.4	3.5	1.1	1.0
Scotland	6.0	11.5	38.5	6.1	5.4	7.4	9.9	2.7	0.9	11.5
Great Britain	7.0	11.5	49.6	6.0	3.6	6.9	9.6	1.6	0.6	3.6

Settlement types and land use

Figure 7.3

Land-use categories by settlement type

The six groups that make up the broadest classes in the ONS scheme (see page 23) represent very different settlement types, but the pattern of urban land use shows remarkable consistency across these groups, as Figure 7.3 shows.

Category of land use	Non-urban	Transport	Residential	Commerce	Industry	Public institutions	Tended open space	Derelict	Transitional	Unsurveyed and Sea
Category nos.	1–10	11	12	13	14	15	16	17	18	19–20
Rural	12.2	9.8	43.5	6.2	4.5	7.2	6.8	2.2	0.6	6.9
Prospering	6.3	9.2	54.8	7.7	3.0	6.7	8.0	1.1	0.3	2.8
Maturer	6.3	10.8	51.6	4.6	2.3	5.8	11.0	1.0	0.4	6.3
Urban centres	7.5	12.8	49.1	5.7	5.7	7.3	9.1	1.6	0.6	0.7
Mining and industrial	6.5	12.9	47.3	5.1	3.3	7.2	10.8	2.5	0.8	3.7
Inner London	5.4	14.3	47.8	10.1	1.6	6.8	10.4	0.8	1.7	1.2
Great Britain	7.0	11.5	49.6	6.0	3.6	6.9	9.6	1.6	0.6	3.6

From our random sample of urban squares, the largest representation is in the mining and industrial type (100 out of 399 squares). However, it is reassuring to see that it is the ONS urban family that comes out closest to our overall pattern of urban land use, with a profile that is very similar to the overall average. The two families described as 'prospering' and 'maturer' are quite similar to each other in most respects, being characterised by above-average proportions of residential land and below-average amounts of transport and industrial land. Examples of such areas occurred in Wokingham, Eastleigh and Bedford (prospering) and in Worthing, Reading and Kingston-upon-Thames (maturer).

In some respects, urban squares in the rural group and those in Inner London might be considered to be at opposite extremes. In fact, the results here show them to be different, but not dramatically different. The proportions of residential, transport and commercial land are higher in Inner London, but the squares in the rural localities have more industry. It should also be remembered that the situation in Inner London, which is unique in some respects, will have a significant bearing upon the regional pattern for the South-East of England.

A few individual categories stand out, but for the most part they tend to confirm, rather than question, initial expectations. For example, the non-urban categories 1–10 are by far the highest in the rural family and the lowest in Inner London, but transport and commercial categories are highest in Inner London. Industrial land is low in all settlement types, reaching a maximum average of only 5.7% in the urban family, and only eight individual squares had more than one-third of their land in industrial use (3 in Birmingham and the Black Country, 2 in Glasgow, 1 each in Runcorn, St Helens and Wellington). Tended open space is lowest in the rural and prospering areas, possibly as a result of easy access from these areas to adjacent countryside and the prevalence of houses with private gardens.

National issues – Task 2

In addition to the basic survey of land-use types in each key square, surveyors were also asked to note the presence or absence of certain specific features. These were chosen in an attempt to shed some light upon particularly topical or contentious environmental issues and to provoke discussion about them. The survey process was deliberately kept simple. The instructions were simply to record the presence or

Photo: A Srokosz

The presence or absence of corner shops: an indicator of local or neighbourhood facilities

absence of the named features in each square. Except for housing, where a group of six was the minimum for inclusion, no numerical or size thresholds were imposed.

The features that were relevant to the survey of urban squares were as follows:

- Housing developments less than five years old (i.e. built in the period 1991–96). This was seen as an indicator of urban growth and the loss of countryside.
- The existence of large supermarkets or hypermarkets. This is a contentious planning issue, especially on the outskirts of many towns.
- The presence of corner shops or village stores: a measure of local or neighbourhood facilities.
- The construction of pylons and communications towers – an increasingly contentious environmental issue.

The fifth designated national issue, setaside farmland, is relevant only to the rural squares.

Task 2 results were returned for 375 urban key squares. Only 26 squares (7%) exhibited none of the named features. On the other hand 20% of the total possessed three out of the four features, and 5% had all four. There was no particular regional bias among these latter squares, but there was an over-representation of settlement families 1 (rural) and 2 (prospering). The results of the Task 2 survey are summarised in Figure 7.4.

It can be seen that approximately three out of every four squares had experienced recent house-building. This is a high level of activity in purely spatial terms, although it is not possible to quantify the numbers of houses involved. Only in the North of England and Scotland did the proportion of squares affected fall substantially below the national average. Particularly high levels were recorded in Wales and East Anglia, although the question of small sample sizes here has already been noted.

The spread of supermarkets/hypermarkets and their association with urban growth and traffic generation has been a contentious issue in many areas. Surveyors were instructed to note the presence of these, but the results, which indicate a presence in over a quarter of all squares, suggest that it is supermarkets of all sizes that have been

Figure 7.4
Task 2 features by region

Region	Housing	Supermarkets	Corner shops	Pylons/towers
North	40.0	26.7	73.3	26.7
Yorkshire and Humberside	84.8	30.3	72.7	21.2
East Midlands	77.3	13.6	72.7	18.2
East Anglia	85.6	42.9	42.9	42.9
South-East	69.0	26.1	69.0	21.2
South-West	81.0	23.8	85.7	9.5
West Midlands	75.7	13.5	86.5	37.8
North-West	81.1	30.2	75.5	20.8
Wales	100.0	25.0	91.7	25.0
Scotland	54.5	36.4	66.7	18.2
Great Britain	**72.8**	**26.1**	**73.3**	**22.7**

recorded. Even so, it is remarkable that this kind of store, which is a product of the last three decades, is now found so frequently. Anybody concerned about the loss of corner shops/general stores, particularly in the face of competition from supermarkets, may be gratified to see that these local shops were recorded in almost three-quarters of the squares surveyed. Particular strongholds were found in Wales, the West Midlands and the South-West.

Electricity pylons and telecommunications towers were recorded in almost a quarter of the squares. Theses features have previously been contentious for their visual impact upon the landscape, but more recently questions have also been raised about their impact upon human health. From the evidence here, they are most common in the West Midlands (and East Anglia on a small sample) and least common in the South-West of England.

Presenting the same information on the basis of settlement type (Figure 7.5) adds a further dimension to our analysis. Interestingly, above-average counts on all four features are found in the urban squares in the rural family, and to a lesser extent in the urban family. If we accept that houses built in the last five years, supermarkets, pylons and telecommunications towers are mainly recent phenomena indicative of urban development, the table can be interpreted as suggesting that small towns have been an important focus of recent urban growth.

This argument is strengthened by the fact that the mining and industrial family, containing settlements unattractive to new investment in recent years, records below-average counts on all four features.

The other settlement type that stands out is Inner London, notably for its low count of new housing. This is understandable because land there for new housing is in short supply, but there may also be other, social, factors at work.

Settlement type	Housing	Supermarkets	Corner shops	Pylons/towers
Rural	79.5	33.3	79.5	30.8
Prospering	81.3	24.0	72.0	24.0
Maturer	68.6	28.6	74.3	20.0
Urban	76.2	28.8	78.8	33.8
Mining and industrial	69.3	19.3	71.6	13.6
Inner London	52.4	33.3	57.1	9.5
Great Britain	**72.8**	**26.1**	**73.3**	**22.7**

Figure 7.5
Task 2 features by settlement type

Conclusion and summary

The survey has produced an interesting and worthwhile set of findings about the contemporary pattern of land use in the urban areas that provide the day-to-day environment for the great majority of the country's population. It reveals that residential land accounts for approximately half the total, equal to all of the other categories of land use combined. Land for transport activities was found to be the second largest category, accounting for approximately one-eighth of the total, and it is interesting to see that transport issues also figured very prominently in the 'views and visions' comments (see Chapter 8). Industry was found to occupy a very small proportion of urban land overall (3.6%), and the category was far outweighed by both public institutions and commercial and business uses. Although land use is only one guide to the economic and social importance of various activities, these findings match other evidence about recent changes in the structure of Britain's urban areas.

There are some regional variations in the patterns, but the differences are not great. The towns of the West and East Midlands are, by a small margin, the most built-up, with over 77% of their land devoted to the core urban activities of residential, transport, commercial and business, and industrial. The proportion of industrial land is above the average only in the West Midlands, the North-West and Scotland.

The results from Task 2, which required surveyors to identify the presence or absence of specific features, showed that three out of every four squares had experienced new house-building since 1990, especially in areas classified as rural or prospering. Supermarkets or hypermarkets were recorded in approximately one-quarter of all the squares, and a similar proportion possessed pylons and communications towers or masts.

We can also draw conclusions relating to the educational value of the exercise. Although these results do not show it directly, it became very evident when examining the returns from the survey teams and talking to some of those involved that the exercise had generated high levels of debate, practical activity and enthusiasm. Those who participated were encouraged to use a large number of academic and personal skills, and learned a great deal about their urban environments.

This chapter provides only an initial analysis of the urban results. The data-set contains much more detail, and will reward further analysis. In addition, the framework is now in place for future, perhaps regular, surveys of the key squares to provide the basis for continuing studies of local changes in land use.

Photo: Tony Dodsworth

Chapter 8: The views and visions of the surveyors

Rex Walford

The third task of the survey was to ascertain the young surveyors' views and visions of the squares which they surveyed. A set of questions was provided in the Survey Pack, together with notes of interpretation and guidance for teachers, who were asked to inform their survey teams of the six questions before they started. Surveyors were asked to make notes about their thoughts while in the field, and then to discuss their responses in a classroom session afterwards. Teachers returned the sheets, having completed them with a consensus opinion and any additional individual responses which seemed of interest.

The analysis of the views and visions sheets needed considerable care, since the responses were free-form and not prompted by any lists of possible answers.

In the time available it has so far been possible only to do preliminary analysis on the returns from 390 urban key squares and 383 rural key squares, a total of 773. Figure 8.1 shows the breakdown of these squares.

	Urban	Rural	Total
England	340	219	559
Scotland	30	123	153
Wales	11	31	42
Northern Ireland	9	10	19
Total	390	383	773

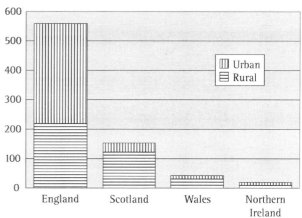

Material from key squares returned after 15 October 1996, and from the 600 local squares, still awaits analysis. It is clear that the wealth of interesting material contained in the 'Task 3 sheets' will repay further study, and it is hoped that further funding can be found for this.

Figure 8.1
Breakdown of the returns

The questions and the responses

Question 1: What single word or short phrase describes best the general character of the square which you have surveyed?

Analysis of this question was carried out in two ways. One approach looked at words which described the square in terms of landscape and townscape form, e.g. *residential*, *rural-urban fringe*, *pastoral*, etc. The second analysed the responses in relation to any qualitative element of the answers, e.g. *remote, bleak, busy*.

Analysis A: landscape and townscape form
Not surprisingly, the term 'residential' featured overwhelmingly in the urban squares (71%).

In the rural squares, there was a greater range of responses, with the most frequently occurring words being 'farmland' (43%), 'heath and moorland' (28%) and 'woodland' (12%).

Analysis B: Qualitative
Here the responses were more varied. Not all of them included a qualitative element. The most frequently used word (synonyms included) in the urban key squares was 'depressing' (16%), closely followed by 'poorly maintained' and/or 'run down' (15%) and, perhaps surprisingly, 'quiet' (13%).

In the rural key squares, the most frequently used words were 'peaceful' and/or 'quiet' (48%), followed by 'remote' (27%) and 'beautiful' (25%).

Overall, in the urban squares 35% of the responses could be counted as **positive**, e.g. 'pleasant', 'friendly', 'elegant', with almost as many (34%) being **negative**, e.g. 'depressing', 'ugly', 'run down', 'unsafe'.

In the rural squares there is a clear difference, with **positive** responses, e.g. 'peaceful', 'beautiful', 'unspoilt', accounting for 61% of the responses and only 29% of responses being **negative**, e.g. 'remote, 'bleak', 'dull'.

Question 2: What things did you find most *interesting* and/or *surprising* in the square?

We have not yet been able to analyse the answers to this question. However, a flavour of the answers is given below:

Interesting
- The volume of new housing in the square – but where are the jobs to match?
- The presence of dwarf willow and shrubs, because there are no deer on the island of Muck
- The scars left by four-wheel-drive vehicles in the countryside
- The importance of grouse-shooting on the maintenance of heather-covered moors
- The OS map indicates boulders and small crags, but on the ground little remains: is this evidence that someone has removed blocks of Westmoreland limestone for use as rockeries?

Surprising
- A pit on the edge of the footpath, where the farmer had been recently burning animal carcasses (a sign of the times?)
- The prefabricated houses, put up immediately after the Second World War, were still occupied.
- Finding hidden features – the Victorian pumping station, the abattoir, the sewing factory, which even 'locals' had not realised were there
- A flat island with high-quality grass: sheep are ferried there by boat to graze
- The unmarked ravine!

Question 3: What do you *like* and *dislike* most about the area which you surveyed?

As with Question 2, we have not yet had the opportunity to analyse the answers to this question. However, this selection gives a good flavour of the answers:

Likes
- The peace and quiet of a classic rural area – a recurring theme in the responses

Photo: Janet Draycott

Increase in the amount of settlement was the predominant vision for both rural and urban environments

- All the paths and alleyways which we discovered we didn't know about
- The harmony of the landscape; lovely views and a rich habitat for wildlife
- The corner shops on the housing estate – they were quaint and friendly
- The pedestrianisation of the High Street has made it a more pleasant place.

Dislikes
- The poor quality of life in the old narrow streets behind the harbour
- The mess left behind by contractors after tree-felling, with no attempt to clear up
- The traffic and the noise-levels, especially the noise from the drop-forge
- The inauthentic street furniture in Chinatown, where they are trying to attract tourists
- Metal shutters on shop fronts, high metal fences: the environment transmits fear of crime.

Question 4: What would you say was the current major environmental *issue* in your square?

A categorisation was first worked out and tested on a pilot number of responses. In some cases, respondents offered more than one issue, but in these cases the analysts sought to identify the most significant of those listed. The leading five issues were the same in both urban and rural key squares.

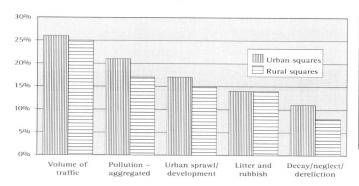

Issue	Urban squares	Rural squares
Volume of traffic	26%	25%
Pollution – aggregated	21%	17%
Urban sprawl (or development)	17%	15%
Litter and rubbish	14%	14%
Decay/neglect/dereliction	11%	8%

Figure 8.2
Leading environmental issues

If traffic issues are aggregated, e.g. traffic volume, traffic noise, exhaust fumes, on-street parking problems and so on, they are mentioned in 44% of urban key square responses and 39% of rural key square responses. **Traffic outnumbered all other broad categories of response by a significant margin.**

Question 5: What *changes*, if any, would you like to see in your square?

As in Questions 1 and 4, a categorisation was first worked out and tested on a pilot number of responses. In this case, if respondents mentioned more than one change, a number of responses (up to three) were coded for each answer. The total number of responses in each category is given in Figure 8.3.

Figure 8.3
Ten leading categories of
changes desired

A large number of rural square respondents (168 out of 347) answered this question by saying that they wished to see 'no change'. Only 12 of 381 respondents who had surveyed urban areas answered 'no change'.

Desired for urban squares		Desired for rural squares	
Improvement in quality of housing	95	Planting or restoration of woodland	57
Improvement in quality of roads	65	Improvement in public access to land	40
Increase in amount of amenities	61	Increase in amount of shops	28
Increase in amount of open space	58	Increase in amount of public transport	26
Improvement of derelict land	33	Increase in amount of amenities	21
Increase in amount of shops	32	Improvement in quality of farming	18
Decrease in amount of traffic	30	Increase in amount of hedgerows	17
Improvement in quality of shops	29	Improvement of derelict land	16
Improvement in quality of open space	23	Improvement in quality of open space	14
Improvement in quality of amenities	20	Decrease in amount of housing	12

Question 6: What is your *vision* of what the square will be like in twenty years' time?

This question is about what the respondents **expect** the square to be like in twenty years' time, not what they **hope** it will be like. Teachers were therefore urged to seek for realism rather than utopianism in their discussions with the survey teams.

As in Question 1, the responses were analysed in two ways:

One analysis looked at the content of the issues that were raised, and followed closely the categorisations developed in considering the responses to Question 5. Multiple responses were registered, up to a maximum of three.

Figure 8.4
Ten leading categories of
visions

The other analysis took a broader view and classified the responses in terms of whether they appeared 'positive', 'negative' or 'neutral' about the future. An 'unclear' category was added for those responses which could not be easily coded into any of the main three. Only one response was registered for each form.

For urban squares		For rural squares	
Increase in amount of settlement	192	Increase in amount of settlement	91
Decrease in amount of open space	126	Increase in amount of tourists	46
Improvement in quality of housing	89	Increase in amount of traffic	41
Increase in amount of traffic	82	Decrease in amount of farmland	36
Decline in quality of housing	46	Decrease in quality of farmland	20
Increase in amount of shops	30	Increase in amount of derelict land	16
Increase in amount of industry	20	Decrease in amount of open space	15
Increase in amount of derelict land	16	Increase in amount of industry	12
Increase in amount of offices	14	Improvement in public access to land	11
Decrease in amount of shops	13	Planting or restoration of woodland	10

Analysis A: Content

A large number of respondents from the rural squares (81) said that their vision was of 'no change'. This was coded as 'neutral' in Analysis B.

Analysis B: Positive or negative visions of the future

It is interesting to note the larger proportion of negative visions which emerged from those groups surveying urban key squares.

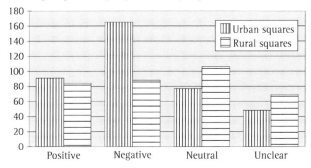

	For urban squares	For rural squares
Positive	91	84
Negative	165	88
Neutral	77	106
Unclear	48	69

Figure 8.5
Positive or negative visions of the future

Some examples of responses given to Question 6 are given below.

From an 8-year-old pupil at St Giles' and St George's Primary School, Newcastle-under-Lyme, Staffordshire, who had surveyed a square in the urban area of the Potteries:

In twenty years' time it will still be urban in Newcastle and there will be more people, more noise and more pollution. The Borough should help to clear up Newcastle, because there is a lot of graffiti and litter around, and it is very dirty. When I am twenty-eight, the Council workmen will probably still be building more roads and widening them, because there are always problems with traffic jams and people are always complaining about them.

From a secondary-school pupil at Ashford High School, Middlesex, who had surveyed an urban square near Heathrow Airport:

I think that in the year 2016 AD our area will be very polluted: all the lakes, rivers and streams will be black with oil pollution. All the empty grassland and fields will be built on with houses, offices and more airport.

From the pupils of Hook Church of England Primary School, near Goole, in Yorkshire, came a consensus view about a rural square near their own village:

In twenty years' time, if we survey the land again, all the fields will have been demolished. Maybe a supermarket and car parks will have been built to cater for all the people in the new housing. Any new houses will be in cul-de-sacs. The houses will have small gardens and will be closely packed together so that more houses can be built in a small area. Due to the growth in population, there will unfortunately be far less wildlife.

From the pupils of Oaklands RC Secondary School, Waterlooville, Hants, a consensus view about an urban square in their town:

We anticipate that any open spaces which currently exist will be built over with new housing.

From the pupils of Winterbourne Junior Girls School, Thornton Heath, Surrey, a consensus view about the suburban square which they surveyed:

In twenty years' time it will be the same, but with more roads and more road humps. Everyone will have a car by then – and it will be total chaos ...

Chapter 9:
Reports from survey teams

compiled by Rex Walford

Besides the value of the results, the Land Use – UK survey was rich in experiences. It was undertaken by students of all ages, from infant schools through to university postgraduates. Teachers with younger children often enlisted the help of local sixth-formers as extra leaders; secondary schools sometimes involved their feeder primary schools and thus forged closer links. Some teachers used the survey as part of their mainstream geography programme: others used it as extension work for the gifted and successful.

The task of surveying was carried out by children in every type of education: those being taught at home; children with learning difficulties from special schools; pupils from day-schools in inner-city areas, in suburbs and in remote rural villages; pupils from comprehensives and prestigious boarding schools alike.

Cressbrook Junior School, near Buxton, has a total school roll of only twelve pupils, but took on the survey of a square. At Whitby Secondary School in Ellesmere Port, on the other hand, the pupils of one year, Year 7, took the leading part in their school's contribution to the survey – all 300 of them!

Survey work took place in school lesson times, in lunch-hours, on Saturday mornings, at half-term and – in the case of the volunteers in the Geographical Task Force – during the summer holidays. One enthusiastic member of the Task Force, John McKeown of Leicester, planned his summer honeymoon location around the key squares he had been given to survey in Scotland. The marriage survives ...

It wasn't only schools and professionals: the Fellside Wolf Cub Pack from near Carlisle organised a cross-border raid to survey a square in the Scottish lowlands; the Antrobus Women's Institute in Cheshire reported that they *thought* they knew their own local environment until they embarked on their survey. Some of the efforts were heroic: first-year undergraduates at the University College of Ripon and York St John surveyed over 120 squares in and around York; Joy Ingram, a member of the Geographical Task Force, surveyed 50 squares in the Highlands on her own.

Recurring themes

In the many letters sent in by teachers, there were constantly recurring themes:

- We were a little apprehensive at first, but it turned out fine.
- The children thoroughly enjoyed it.
- The pupils gained a great deal – map-skills were improved, knowledge of the locality was gained.
- I anticipate the spin-offs will be as important as the survey itself.
- It was surprising to find X (or Y or Z) in our square – although this is our local area, we didn't know it was there.

- This has provoked much discussion about the environment in our class.
- We felt proud to be part of a national project.
- Our intention is to repeat this in subsequent years.

Extracts from surveyors' reports

Here are some extracts from just some of the reports:

Photo: Western Daily Press

Press and TV coverage in Bath

Twenty-five Year-11 girls did the survey – a most interesting and valuable day which all enjoyed and, I suspect, a useful marketing tool for A-level take-up next term. We had two reports and a picture in the Bath Chronicle, *and BBC South-West sent out a camera crew for the day and produced a 3-minute clip on local TV. There was a longer report on BBC Radio Bristol. All in all, an excellent day out with good publicity for the GA and our school.*

Marilyn Cass, Head of
Geography, The Royal School, Bath

Cliff challenge in Orkney

Our last square (319,1004) was particularly difficult to access, involving a return boat trip and steep climbs to the top of 300-metre-high sea cliffs facing the Atlantic. However, the pupils found the survey challenging and thoroughly enjoyed doing this square in particular.

Ralph Harnden, Head of Geography, Stromness Academy, Orkney

Carrying on tradition in Oxfordshire

I am a retired geography teacher who helps out, on a part-time basis, at Combe C of E Primary School, Oxon. The exercise was very valuable to the children – mapwork: setting maps in the field, use of compass, etc. – good training for further fieldwork when they go on to secondary school. Time was the problem, especially with other pressures on trying to cover all that is in the National Curriculum. The Headteacher was most supportive and enthusiastic and gave me as much time as she was able. I have also had good support from Mr John Forster, the Education Officer for Blenheim Estates, who enabled us to go onto the Duke of Marlborough's land where we could not cover by normal access.

Having also surveyed for Professor Coleman's 1962 Land Utilisation Survey and having been a pupil at Northampton Grammar School (where the Head of Geography was Dr E. E. Field who originated the 1928 Northamptonshire survey which first attracted Dudley Stamp's attention), I have been so pleased and honoured to have a hand in this venture. Thank you for the detailed planning and advice given in your Survey Pack; it was really helpful and valuable. P. B. Cartwright, Witney, Oxfordshire

Geography club 1

The work was undertaken by a group of 20 volunteers from Years 7 to 9 on a Saturday morning. Follow-up has taken place at a lunchtime 'Geography Club'. They enjoyed the mapping immensely and their work was surprisingly accurate.

David Streets, Head of Geography, Hitchin Boys School, Hertfordshire

Geography club 2

A group of ten Year-5 pupils completed the survey of our square. We formed a Geography Club and met every Tuesday for approximately an hour and a half a week in the months of June and July. Our next aim of the Club is to get together with our local comprehensive school and complete an exhibition with them, ready for Geography Action Week.

R Cromie, Grange County Junior School, Runcorn

Photo: R Cromie

Third time for Marlborough

We have undertaken a large display showing the work of the College in both this and the two earlier surveys of the 1960s and the 1930s. This display was seen over our Prize Weekend, and will remain up during the Summer School, which attracts several hundred members.

Christopher Joseph, Head of Geography, Marlborough College, Wiltshire

Lancashire – involving the families

The whole exercise has created much interest. We notified the parents of key stage 2 children about the work to be undertaken and twelve families expressed interest in being involved. I then divided our square into twelve areas and produced maps showing each of them, together with a breakdown of the key and details of what each category consists of. We held a meeting early one evening to which the families were invited. I was then able to distribute the pack of materials and clipboards and answer any queries.

The work was carried out during the weekend of 29–30 June: a weekend of horrendous wind and rain! However, the results were all safely returned to school on Monday 1 July. Since then I have collated the results, helped by Year 6. It has proved to be an enjoyable and informative exercise for the young people concerned, and the family involvement means that we have been able to share our findings with a wider audience.

Janet Hetherington, Geography Co-ordinator, Staining Primary School, Lancashire

Duke of Edinburgh scheme contribution

The survey was completed as part of the school's Duke of Edinburgh Award expedition and was ideal as 'purpose work' for the students. Many thanks for organising the survey so efficiently.

M. R. Watkins, Great Cornard Upper School, Suffolk

Fieldwork for a special group in London

Home-educated children of several different ages in this area have helped in the survey, which was very worthwhile ... each group of mappers was given an enlarged copy of the square on a clipboard, with their personal route highlighted in gold felt-tip pen. After the field-trip, the children took their own mapped routes and translated them into new clean copies. Each wanted his own personal copy. I went back to complete the master map on several occasions after work and at the weekend. I had several letters from impressed parents afterwards. All in all a very worthwhile exercise. Thanks for all your work.

Shaun Hexter, East London EO Group

Midlands enthusiasm

Thank you for organising this special event. It has been an extremely worthwhile task for my 7/8-year-old children and one which they will remember for a long time. We also discovered lots of things about our immediate neighbourhood which we had not known before, and it was much more fun to develop geographical vocabulary and mapping skills out in the field than behind a desk!

Mrs J Redstall, St Anne's First School, Bewdley, Worcestershire

Children's perspectives from Northumberland

- *I think the land-use survey was a really good idea because people can learn things they did not know and my group thoroughly enjoyed it.*
- *It was good because we stroked the horses.*
- *I liked it because we smelled the flowers.*
- *It was good, because there was more countryside than I thought.*
- *It was good, because you get to miss school.*

Children of Year 6, Guide Post Middle School, Chippington, Northumberland

Thorough approach in Cambridge

This was a thoroughly enjoyable and valuable exercise. The support material has been excellent and we are looking forward very much to the end product. The survey was undertaken by a group of 26 Year-7 pupils of high ability, divided into four sub-groups. The field observations were very good ... they each produced an individual report ... we spent three or four hours of lesson time in discussing and collating the information, plus individual homework time, to produce the reports and an exhibition of the survey for school Open Day. The pupils enjoyed the 'views and visions' section the most; there was a very lively discussion in class, with some excellent perception and evaluation.

Jane Whitehead, Head of Geography, Perse Girls School, Cambridge

Special-needs involvement

Our completed map was carried out by a group of nine Year-10 pupils with moderate learning difficulties under close supervision. I am very proud of their achievement. Having questioned them closely I am sure they have gained a great deal of pleasure and some knowledge from the experience.

M. Leighton, Deputy Head, Halesbury School, Halesowen

Photo: Cumberland News, Carlisle

Preparing the next generation – Cumbria

It has been a very enjoyable and useful project. It has made the children look more closely at their environment and think about what may happen to it. That is important because they are the next generation who will make decisions about how much land will be used for buildings and roads and how much will remain as countryside.

Gill Silson, Geography Co-ordinator, Ivegill School, Cumbria

Perfect opportunity for a field-studies centre

The survey for our key square was completed on July 11th by six Year-12 students from Barking Abbey Comprehensive School as part of their A-level fieldweek. Thank you for providing such a well-planned and worthwhile exercise!

Malcolm Mason, Trewern Outdoor Education & Field Studies Centre, Hay-on-Wye

Maximising opportunities in Gloucester

Before going out into our kilometre square with our Year-4 children, I introduced the idea of land being used for different purposes by looking at a plan of our own school and grounds. We shaded in the plan of the school according to its different uses after discussing such uses as:

- *Industry – classrooms/work areas*
- *Transport – the entrance hall/corridors*
- *Commercial and business uses – offices/tuck shop/kitchen*
- *Tended open space – playing field/playground*

We then walked out into our square for two separate days of surveying. At certain locations we stopped to give places a score for the following range of qualities:

- *attractive/OK/not attractive*
- *welcoming/OK/unwelcoming*
- *interesting/OK/uninteresting*
- *colourful/OK/dull*
- *tidy/OK/untidy*
- *peaceful/OK/noisy*
- *busy/OK/deserted*
- *clean/OK/ dirty*

A score was calculated for each place and it was then given a label of **ugly, plain, ordinary, pleasing** *or* **outstanding.** *We made observations at three different residential sites, and on the main road at two different locations.*

On the second of our survey days we were invited to the Gloucester Royal Hospital by the General Manager of Children's and Women's Services. We were given a conducted tour of the hospital site and allowed to view our survey square from the 10th floor of the main building. The children found this really exciting!

They were also very interested in the different land uses within the hospital site and were able to assess contrasting places such as the front entrance, the main concourse and the gardens, using the same qualities as those listed above. Interestingly, by far the majority of the children voted for 'outstanding' for all three places. The General Manager, Mr Byrne, was quite impressed by how the visit went and we are hoping to develop the link with the hospital in the future, possibly producing some cross-curricular teacher/pupil resources for other schools to use.

Lots of photographs were taken and I am looking forward to mounting a display of all the work that the children did as part of Land Use – UK during Geography Action Week in November – including the delightful letters that two hospital cleaning ladies wrote to the children, remarking on how many times we had walked over their beautiful clean floor!

I was initially quite anxious about children so young undertaking such a survey but I must confess that they all really enjoyed the tasks and coped very well indeed – both out in the square and back in class afterwards. Thank you for the opportunity to use 'real live geography'.

Val Harris, Geography Co-ordinator, Kingsholm Primary School, Gloucester

Enthusiasm and economy – Hemel Hempstead

Thank you for letting us take part in the national Land Use – UK survey. We have felt really proud to be part of something so important that has been happening all over the country. We are a class of thirty-one Year 5 and 6 pupils, so a lot of us will soon be going on to secondary schools. We will be able to tell our geography teachers there all about it.

We thought the instructions were really clear. It was good to learn how to produce an accurate map and the percentage figures. We enjoyed the discussion about the issues and were surprised to find that on the whole we were very much agreeing with each other about trends here and how they fit with national issues. It was interesting to see the map taking shape as we began to colour it in; we sawed the crayons in half so that we could share them better.

The pupils of Mrs McCall's class, Chambersbury Primary School,
Hemel Hempstead

A-level bridge

Well done, team! You have successfully alerted us to the tremendous resource that has always existed close to the school: the local area! This survey has convinced my colleagues of the potential of very local fieldwork. We used the survey as a bridge between two modules of the AEB A-level.

Patrick Talbot, Geography Department, Hampton School, Middlesex

Close-up in Middlesbrough

Survey of our allocated square by Year-9 pupils opting for geography next year proved a most valuable exercise from the following points of view:

- *It sharpened their observation skills through looking closely and critically at the area surrounding the college.*
- *Features which were familiar to the point where students had ceased to notice them were thrown into new focus and gained interest.*
- *The survey provided a tremendous motivational force for the start of the students' GCSE course.*
- *It focused attention on the relevance and use of geography in general.*

Mrs C. Gilchrist, Head of Geography, Macmillan CTC, Middlesbrough

Rescue and romance around Maidstone

The Year-9 and Year-10 Corners groups (13 boys and 5 girls) joined forces to survey the two areas of land adjacent to the school. On the second day, one team helped in the rescue of a lost dog; they managed to find its owner and everyone was happy. Romance bloomed between two group members during the survey, so remember – geography can lead to love ...

From the newsletter of The Cornwallis School, Maidstone

Praise for variety

The students really enjoyed the surveying. Had we had just one square the results would have been completed easily, but teams of students were responsible for different squares for their Local Studies Duke of Edinburgh's Award Skills Section and so the collation was more difficult. But we are pleased with the variety in the squares – this has promoted much discussion – **thanks!**

Nicky Edie, Head of Geography, Ashcroft High School, Luton

From St Albans to a worthwhile exercise in Luton

We surveyed two areas of Luton on the 4th of July amidst true fieldwork weather – drizzle. In order to do the survey in an area ten miles away, I did a visit beforehand and, at the same time, dropped information into all the schools and premises we might need to cross. This was very useful and often the school knew a lot about local changes. In many cases I wondered why they had not opted to take part in the survey.

I selected 28 bright Year-9 boys (we are a boys' school) and obtained the help of three prefects and another geographer. This allowed us to use two minibuses and, since we had two key squares, a teacher in charge of each area. The task took less time than expected. There was, however, a need to check the maps carefully since many found it difficult relating a building on the map to one they were surveying. Any problems were quickly solved in the spare time and it also allowed us to colour-code the maps on the same day while everything was fresh.

The total write-up took about 4 hours, with some tasks being completed at home by enthusiastic members of the teams. We took photos of the area and of the fieldwork in action and used these in our display. We have composed a letter for our 'linked' school and will send them copies of the results. I checked the maps and did go back to resolve issues in some areas where there were discrepancies.

The discussions were very interesting. The Biscot area was very Asian in one half and appeared an inner-city area. However, the other side of the square revealed an area which had few shops – maybe a reflection of affluence and car ownership.

Stopsley was middle-class with one council estate and no great ethnic-minority presence apparent in any section. Our school pupils come from a relatively affluent area: it certainly opened their eyes to other areas and made them think about similarities which may exist in St Albans.

All-in-all a worthwhile exercise. We are even thinking of adapting it for local Year-8 fieldwork and will use the Biscot area of Luton, in future, for sixth-form work on issues related to segregation in cities. I have used the maps with Year 10 to look at types of housing on maps as part of their settlement study. We are hoping to display our results in the library and have contacted the papers. We will contact them again when we have the main results. We look forward to receiving these, and are pleased to think that we have helped in a small way.

Nicki Marriott, Verulam School, St Albans, Hertfordshire

Adversity in Lincolnshire

Here at last is our completed survey. It was quite eye-opening to see the relative proportions of residential and grassland emerging as we completed it. We have all thoroughly enjoyed carrying out the survey and the Year-6 children learned many useful skills – not least, patience in adversity, plus the need for a lot of co-operation! I am looking forward to continuing the work next year, as the new Year-6 group follow up the results and exchange information with our twinned school in Essex.

Lindsey Sutton, North Kelsey County Primary School, Lincolnshire

A pattern established for future years

The survey took place on 17 and 18 June with Year-7 pupils (about 280 in total) assisted by Year-12 pupils. We all enjoyed the exercise and the response of the pupils was excellent. We intend to repeat the exercise on a smaller scale in future years and hope to undertake a similar exercise on Anglesey when the incoming Year-7 pupils go on a week-long visit. We have also visited one of our feeder primaries to help them complete their mapping and Task 3 in the area around their school, as part of our primary liaison programme.

Ms A. Crossley, Head of Geography, Whitby County High School, Ellesmere Port

A useful map-reading exercise

The survey was undertaken by a mixed group of Year-7 and Year-8 pupils over one and a half days during the last week of term. It proved to be a very useful map-reading exercise as pupils had to think about where they were in order to record their results. The survey provided us with a valuable opportunity to get to know our neighbourhood and our staff assisting realised how easy it is to ignore our immediate surroundings when cocooned in our motor cars.

Mrs S. J. Wood, Hammond School, Chester

Overseas involvement

In itself, the exercise was a fascinating geographical experience. The children learned more about the area around school by doing this than they have over several years of being driven daily to and from it. The processing of the information was really interesting and valuable too.

Jackie Kirk, Brussels English Primary School, Belgium

Strong support from the Isle of Wight

The class of Year-4 children enjoyed the whole experience from the survey phase through to the follow-up mapping and data analysis. They have gained a much deeper insight into their local environment and have been challenged by the work involved. They will remember their participation in such an important national event over many years to come.

Staff have also valued the experience in adding to their understanding, not only of our local area, but also the methodology in carrying out 'real life' geography. The work will be useful in adding to our future curriculum.

Mrs H. V. Maher, Headteacher, Whippingham County Primary School, Isle of Wight

Sponsorship success

I decided to make the event a significant one by incorporating it as one of the options for our Activities Week. The survey tasks were aimed at Years 7–9 in this, an 11–18 school. Over 50 students opted to help with the survey over three days. Around a dozen Year-11 and A-level geography students volunteered to come back into school after their examinations to act as group leaders for the younger students and improve all safety aspects.

I then contacted the local press, issued a press release to them, and they are coming to visit the school during the event to run a story. School certificates have been designed and printed for all students taking part.

I telephoned a few companies that were sympathetic towards the school (guided by the Parents Association), asking if they would sponsor the Geography Department to purchase some clipboards for the survey. After one or two disappointments, I was delighted that Zurich Municipal (the school's insurers – we are a GM school) agreed to purchase 100 clipboards with 'Oaklands Geography' and 'Zurich Municipal' names on. These will be presented just before the survey takes place.

So, therefore, simply by using Land Use – UK not only as a very useful activity in its own right but as a major event:
- *The profile of geography has been raised in many year groups.*
- *The senior management team and school governors are aware that we are taking part in a national event.*
- *We have gained 100 clipboards for use in all future geography field trips.*
- *The nature of the local area has been put into perspective for many students. It has been quite a challenge to co-ordinate all of the spin-off but well worth*

*it. The survey pack was very useful in this respect. We look forward to the
publication of the results.*

J. W. Lomas, Head of Geography, Oaklands RC School and Sixth Form College,
Waterlooville, Hampshire

Buzzed by the sheikh's helicopter

*The land in one of our survey squares in
Ross-shire, the huge deer forest of
Killilan, is owned by Sheikh Mohammed
of Dubai, better known for his success as
a horse-breeder and racer. The landscape
itself is very striking with many glacial
features and a real feeling of remoteness.
It was quite something to experience the
feeling of being among true wilderness.*

Photo: Jeremy Krause

*My daughter, Julia, and I were out
surveying in the late afternoon and early
evening and were the only people in the
area for much of the time. Only the deer
were there to watch us from a distance, as
an eagle swooped overhead. Then a
helicopter (part of the management of the
deer and deer-shoots) 'buzzed' us.*

Jeremy Krause (Chester), a member of the
Geographical Task Force

Great media coverage in Caterham

*During the project we were interviewed by a reporter from Southern Counties
Radio, who recorded the views of the pupils, aged 6 and 7, about their survey of
the local area. He asked them to think about the changes they thought might
happen in the area in the next 20 years. This was broadcast at 6.00 am and
8.30 am on Monday 10 June.*

On 9 July, Trevor Lawson, a reporter from the Geographical Magazine, *came
out with us when we were actually involved in the land-use survey of our local
square.*

*The children have produced a portfolio of photographs, illustrations and
thank-you letters for distribution to the national sponsors of the project. We
have produced another portfolio of work which is to be sent to the school with
which we have twinned in Carmarthen.*

Laraine Poulter, Head Teacher, St Peter and St Paul Primary School, Caterham

Bridgwater focus on urban decay

*Our square was located on a large council estate built in the 1930s for the
workforce of British Cellophane. 16,000 people were employed by BC in the
1970s; today only 600. A Clarks Shoes factory (also in the square) was
demolished in the 1980s and 700 jobs lost. There are huge problems –
vandalism, youth unemployment, etc. We did research into the work of the
Single Regeneration Budget, about to spend £8 million in the area. Mr John
Andrew, leader of SRB, came to speak to the children of the problems, the
issues and the way forward. Many significant issues were discussed and the
children took part in a role-play exercise to plan the future of the local area.*

*We contacted Bridgwater College and recruited 30 A-level geography
students to join our 120 Year 5 and 6 children to help with Land Use – UK.
Twenty adult helpers and four staff also helped. Excellent co-operation all*

round. The survey was a really useful exercise. The staff, initially underwhelmed when the apparently unpromising urban square was first located, felt that the whole episode was an invaluable exercise. We were reported in the local paper and on local radio.

Moira Daggar, Eastover Primary School, Bridgwater, Somerset

Keen participation in West Yorkshire

The survey was undertaken by a group of Year-9 students ... who thoroughly enjoyed their day and participated in the survey with great enthusiasm, especially when the local press arrived to take their photographs – which appeared in The Morley Observer, The Morley Advertiser *and* The Wakefield Express. *We had a lot of positive feedback from the pupils, most of whom were fascinated to visit areas of their home town which they had not visited before. Their enthusiasm for the survey was so great that many interviewed members of the public and shopkeepers, even though they were not encouraged to do so, in order to complete the national issues and 'views and visions' forms. We have enjoyed participating in the survey – it was a valuable educational experience.*

R. W. Saunders, Woodkirk High School, Tingley, West Yorkshire

Photo: R W Saunders

Lots of spin-offs from a Devon survey

We fitted the survey in at the end of June, after public and school exams. The Lower Sixth were chosen as our surveyors and they managed well, gaining first-hand experience of surveying techniques, as well as a useful insight into the changes affecting rural Devon. We found the instructions thorough and helpful, even though we were unable to attend a training session. We enjoyed the idea of being part of a national project and, since beginning the study, the Head of Geography has been interviewed on local radio (Lantern FM), there has been a short (if inaccurate) account of the survey in our local newspaper and we may be featured in a documentary about the landscape of Devon which is being produced by BBC South-West. There has also been a good deal of interest shown in geography by colleagues and friends.

Our two squares were both remote rural areas, but we were surprised by the contrasts between them. The first square seemed deserted, if not abandoned, and we immediately assumed rural depopulation problems caused by its inaccessibility (if not something more lurid and sinister!). Then, just round the corner, in the other half of our square, we found a growing golf and country club with residential chalets ... there were extensive Forestry Commission plantations of conifers, but part of these seemed to have been cleared and the land added to the golf course.

At first glance our second square seemed typical of rural mid-Devon. There was a small dairy farm on undulating land near Dartmoor, with most of its acreage devoted to grass. However, the neighbouring farm was now owned by a London commuter (London is about 200 miles away). His wife uses the farm to breed red setters, while the farm fields were being planted with trees. Government grants, the dairy farmer told us, were available for this. He also pointed out the great impact of government policy on rural land use. We thought that he might deplore this use of agricultural land for trees, but to our amazement he told us that, in the past, the whole district had been more wooded. Thus, we discovered that both our squares illustrated the changes taking place in the British countryside.

Miss N. Norris, Edgehill College, Bideford, Devon

Coventry – more A-level involvement

Photo: Finham Park School,Coventry

Our Sixth Form undertook the survey work as an introduction to the Enquiry Module for the Cambridge Modular A-level. The timing, at the beginning of July, after their first option module exam, was ideal for this. The fieldwork took place in A-level induction week, so potential Sixth Form geographers were able to get involved too. In fact we have decided to survey the grid square in which the school is located in the next year and possibly involve the local primary school too. In subsequent years we'll move on to neighbouring squares and involve other partner primary schools. Over time we hope to build up an interesting pattern of land use around the school, as well as primary-school links.

Terri Collins, Head of Geography and Co-ordinator for Environmental Education, Finham Park School, Coventry

Juniors to study the coalfields

I would like to take this opportunity to say how much my class and the adults who accompanied us on the trip enjoyed taking part in the survey. I feel that the children gained a lot from this opportunity, particularly in map-reading skills and in the raising of their awareness of environmental issues. The presence of a disused colliery in our key square did prove to be of particular interest to the children and I would hope that, as a school, we will be able to track any future development of the site.

Julia Green, Bawtry Mayflower Junior and Infants School, Bawtry, Doncaster

Photo: Bawtry Mayflower School

Sussex: Action Week plans

My class of Year-3 and Year-4 children thoroughly enjoyed carrying out the survey, especially as I enlisted the help of Simon Rowe, Head of Geography at Tideway Sixth Form College, and his A-level geography students. Here are some of the children's comments:

Kendall*: I certainly would do geography again, it was fun.*

Nicky*: I learned how to do geography and how to write things down on a map.*

Teresa*: We saw some pylons and some surprising things – like new buildings,* *where on the map was just an empty space. I like geography because I like working with people.*

As a follow-up I have planned to run a 'pre-Geography Action Week' focus at the annual governors-report-to-parents evening in October. I hope then to present the survey results with site photographs, children's work and videos of the survey. During Action Week itself, each class will be working on separate ideas chosen from the '101 ideas' pack, after discussion at staff meetings in the early part of the autumn term. We appeared on Meridian TV on 15 July. We have certainly raised the profile of geography in our school and had fun in the process.

Betty Murgatroyd, Denton County Primary School, Newhaven, Sussex

Certificates of achievement

Using the blank poster-heading sent in the mailing, I produced a certificate for each of our six survey-team members for inclusion in their record of achievement folder. These are to be presented by the Head during a geography lesson.

Yvonne Magson, Bexhill High School, Sussex

Small can be beautiful

We are a tiny village school with only 12 pupils, aged 4–11 years. All the children of the school were involved in the survey and all gained a great deal from their involvement. Parents, governors and other villagers showed interest and enthusiasm for the project. We had some excellent publicity in two local newspapers, which we hope will attract attention to the good work done in the school and maybe encourage other parents living nearby to enrol their children here.

Shirley Johnson, Cressbrook Primary School, near Buxton, Derbyshire

Extending the survey in Kent

We enjoyed the fieldwork and will be undertaking additional squares for our own reference in school over the next 12 months. We will be talking about this at the AGM of the Kent Geography Teachers Association this autumn and possibly hope to pool results in the county into a survey pack for Kent schools.

Malcolm Wright, Head of Geography, The Hayesbrook School, Tonbridge

Putney's survey spans the Thames

We had no problems doing the survey which we carried out on two separate days. North of the Thames was done with our entire Year 7 (90 students) with the help of 10 members of staff, some of whom were student teachers at the Institute of Education in London. We also used our A-level geographers to watch over and help Year 7, who definitely felt they had achieved something of national significance. South of the river was done by our A-level geographers with the help of two members of staff. Because of the large expanses of derelict land and industry we decided this area was wholly unsuitable for Year 7s or large groups to survey; the A-level geographers did it admirably.

In all cases a 70-minute lesson was spent outlining and preparing what had to be done in the field. Another 70-minute lesson was spent following up Tasks 2 and 3 and doing a write-up for this section. A final 70-minute lesson was spent completing the colouring of the land-use map.

For all the fieldwork we worked from recent (1992) 1:1 250 OS maps that I obtained from Wandsworth Council, which made the recording of the different land uses easy as many of the changes were marked clearly. We experienced no problems in transferring the information down onto the 1:10 000 maps, In fact,

I found this a very useful lesson to do with Year 7 as part of their map-skills unit. All stages went well and this was largely due to plenty of extra time being built into the Year 7 scheme of work and to your helpful advice. Thank you for taking so much time and trouble to ensure the smooth running of this really magnificent project.

Vanessa Owston, Geography Department, Putney High School, London

Enjoyment for mixed age groups

We are a small two-teacher school with approximately 50 pupils and despite a few second thoughts about taking part in the project when the initial survey pack arrived, we decided to go ahead. Our numbers and staffing meant working with mixed groups of 6–9-year-old children, which in fact proved beneficial for all concerned. Perhaps most importantly we have enjoyed the whole process. Thank you for the detailed information pack and support materials which have been an enormous help in planning the work with the children.

Jackie Scott, Headteacher, Whittingham C of E School, Northumberland

Follow-up planned in Worcestershire

The survey task was given to a class of Year-3 children as they were doing a local study at the time. We were initially a little apprehensive as to whether the children would cope, but with guidance given by the class teacher they were able to complete the survey successfully. They learned a great deal about different land uses and were able to put their map-reading skills into a practical context ... our intention now is to follow this survey in subsequent years by identifying any changes, and we also intend to extend the area.

D. R. Smith, Geography Co-ordinator, Belle Vue Primary School,
Wordsley, Worcestershire

Team effort in Southampton

In the middle of a lovely hot July day, four of us set off to map our local grid square. We became involved due to the rural nature of our Individual Study Module for our geography A-levels. We learned how to use a nationally recognised method of land-use surveying and had a thoroughly nice time – the boys mapping the northern half of the grid square by bike, the girls covering the south on foot. Our work will be referred to in years to come – which gives us all a sense of pride in what we have done.

Jenny Hayball, Sixth Form student at
Taunton's College, Southampton

Photo: Taunton's College, Southampton

Practical geography – Devon

I have a class of Years 4, 5 and 6, and I selected children from each of these year groups to take part. Each group was led by a sixth-year pupil and an adult. The square we were given was very interesting and the farmer who owns most of the land was very co-operative and keen to contribute. As you will see from our 'views and visions' form, he is taking advantage of government subsidies and some of the farm buildings have been converted into 'gites' through grants from the RDC.

The survey was a great success and particularly as we could climb up above Great Leigh Farm and look down on the area we had surveyed. We could incorporate the whole idea of how the land looks from above and how maps are made. Anne Jones, Christow Primary School, near Exeter, Devon

Photo: P W Thomas

Welsh gold

The survey was undertaken by a group of Year-10 pupils and the students responded to the work in a very positive manner. The work was conducted throughout in the medium of Welsh, including conversations with the three landowners whose land covered the square.

One whole day was given to the survey in addition to much further time analysing and recording the results. Britain's most commercially viable gold mine lies 1.2 km to the south-west of our square and test drillings have taken place within the confines of the square itself.

P. W. Thomas, Ysgol y Gader, Dolgellau, Gwynedd, Wales

Mixed ages and cross-curricular possibilities

We found the land-use survey an extremely worthwhile and useful activity which really made us focus on the square kilometre in detail. The 'views and visions' form generated very mature discussion among the 10- and 11-year-old children. Ours is a mixed-age class of 20 children between the ages of 7 and 11, but there was sufficient variety within the task to generate plenty of differentiation. The cross-curricular possibilities are great and I foresee this being a regular activity within our planning scheme.

Gwyneth Alban, Headteacher, Ysgol Gynradd Alltwalis, Dyfed, Wales

International aspirations

Our day in the field was a great success. It did not fit into our schemes of work for this term or existing fieldwork, and therefore became a task for a group of students from across the school who had been identified as having done well in geography this year. Placed in a new grouping and taken out of school, these pupils worked very well together and produced excellent discussion on their return to school ... for me it was valuable to hear the pupils articulate how useful they found fieldwork to be in their learning in geography.

Carrying on from this project I will be representing my school in Albuquerque, USA, at the conference of the Coalition of Essential Schools in the autumn. I will be making a presentation about my pupils' involvement in the land-use survey and hoping to establish links with schools in the USA which would be prepared to carry out similar exercises so that we can compare results at an international level.

Sara Wright, Hugh Christie Technology Centre, Tonbridge, Kent

A co-operative group in Northumberland

A Year-5 class, four members of staff, two parents and several work-experience students from the High School undertook this survey. We all enjoyed it; it was very good experience for Year 5 and it has fired them with enthusiasm for geography topics in the future.

Mrs M. Wilson, Geography Co-ordinator, Parkside Middle School, Cramlington, Northumberland

Hot fieldwork at Hurst

Although the survey took a lot of time, we found it a worthwhile experience. At our school it was done with thirty pupils from Year 4. We went out for four days for periods of about an hour in groups of up to ten pupils. It was hot and tiring, but the children remarked that there were things that they had never noticed before. The activity has certainly expanded my knowledge in geography and I hope to share it with my colleagues, so as to enhance fieldwork at Hurst. We all thank you for giving us the opportunity to participate in such an invaluable and rewarding experience.

Patricia Tandoh, Geography Co-ordinator, Hurst Primary School, Bexley, Kent

Land-use surveyors to the rescue

We did the survey with Year 6. We have enjoyed being part of the survey and while out in the field we were even called on to provide a group effort to rescue a lamb stuck in a fence!

Jane Murray, Kirkoswald School, near Penrith, Cumbria

Land Use – UK joins the Eisteddfod

The National Eisteddfod of Wales was, in 1996, situated west of the village of Ffairfach near Llandeilo in the valley of the River Towy [or in Land Use – UK terms Local Square 262,221]. 'Gwaith Maes' planned a programme of activities in the Science Pavilion all week: one activity involved surveying the square.

During the week, one lady approached us who was involved in the very first Land Utilisation Survey.

Olive Dyer, Trinity College, Carmarthen

Cymdeithas Gwaith Maes

Photo: O A Dyer

Great co-operation in a changing area

As the square was located in Chesterfield, a 45-minute minibus journey from school, we were greatly relieved when Chesterfield Urban Studies Centre not only provided us with a base, but also opened its doors and extensive resources to us ... it made up-to-date video materials and local information available and we studied these in the morning of our survey day.

In all, we calculated that over 40% of the square had changed since the original survey of the 1930s, and in the most dramatic of ways.

The children worked very well throughout the survey and we all worked hard collecting and interpreting the information. Thankfully, we found the quarry company, local inhabitants, Derbyshire County Council Engineers Department and Chesterfield Urban Studies Centre extremely co-operative. The survey was an intriguing exercise of immeasurable educational value to both the children and the adults involved.

J. Langley-Fogg, Derwent Community School, Derby

Last word

Eight-year-old Kendall, from Denton Primary School in Eastbourne, showed the potential for a new generation of geographers:

I would like to do geography again – it was fun!

Photo: Aylesbury High School

A 'twinning' visit: Dave
Eddon of Kyle Academy
with Jane Brownlee and
students of Aylesbury
High School

Chapter 10:
The twinning experience

Moreen Morron

Twinning is a working partnership between teachers and their classes in different schools, providing an exciting vehicle for promoting greater knowledge and understanding of their own and another area. Communicating directly enables pupils to explore two environments from first-hand data, and the exchange of information and experiences disseminates good educational practice and fosters the development of genuine partnerships. Another major benefit of twinning for pupils is the recognition that their home area is interesting to outsiders, thus increasing their self-esteem.

An important feature of Land Use – UK was the opportunity it provided for schools to twin with a school in another part of the country. The National Steering Committee decided at an early stage in the planning of the survey that schools should be encouraged to twin, believing that this activity would make a significant contribution to the National Curriculum requirement that pupils should study a contrasting locality. Involvement with real people and places helps deliver exciting geography, and the vast majority of the participants in Land Use – UK asked to be twinned – in all, 1100 schools, colleges and outdoor centres welcomed the chance to forge links with another group involved in this historic survey.

Pat Partington and I, and Diane Wright from the GA staff, accepted responsibility for organising the twinning. We used information from the UK postcode map as a basis for establishing contrasts, together with the geographical knowledge of the organisers and anyone else in the immediate vicinity! It was far from being an exact science, but we did attempt to link schools in contrasting localities – in the main, we twinned according to educational phase, urban with rural, inland with coastal, north with south, and, as far as we could, English schools were twinned with schools in Northern Ireland, Scotland and Wales. We had to start the twinning process before all the applications for squares were in, so we adopted a 'best fit' solution for each batch of schools, but wherever possible we accommodated individual requests for partners. During the spring of 1996 we became very familiar indeed with the map of UK postcodes at the GA in Sheffield, and by 31 May all twinned schools had been notified.

We did not wish to be prescriptive (nor did we in any case have the resources for a heavy involvement in the twinned schools' activities) so we confined our advice to the suggestion that statistics, maps and the pupils' views and visions should be exchanged.

How did they get on? What follows is a description of the experiences of twinned schools in various parts of the UK. Each partnership is unique, and some very diverse outcomes were to be expected. In describing some of these outcomes we hope to celebrate this diversity, the wealth of creativity demonstrated by teachers and the enthusiastic involvement of the children: it was an unequivocal success.

Harthill and Nunthorpe

Harthill, a small rural primary school in Cheshire, twinned with Nunthorpe, a suburban primary school in Cleveland. To start with, both schools located the places of birth of their teachers and pupils on a map of the UK, and the children exchanged letters. Catherine, from Harthill, told Kylie in Nunthorpe that she had been born in Ashby-de-la-Zouch, but she expected Kylie had never heard of it. 'You're right,' replied Kylie, 'I had not heard of Ashby-de-la-Zouch *ever* before, but my teacher passes through it on the way to her parents in Gloucestershire. I've looked it up in the atlas.' Christopher, from Nunthorpe, wrote: 'The wonderful North-East will have three teams in the premiership – Sunderland, Newcastle and Middlesbrough. Can you find them on the map?' Letter/number co-ordinates and four-figure grid-reference skills were developed by this activity, and finding places related to real children elsewhere made it exciting and purposeful. They used a road atlas to establish the route between the two schools, and a sequence of photographs was exchanged and annotated by the recipients.

Both schools are aiming to be Eco-schools and are involved in Local Agenda 21 initiatives. Action plans on saving energy and recycling paper were exchanged by the pupils, who commented on letters which were written on only one side of the paper: a technology lesson in how to photocopy on both sides ensued.

Harthill sent Nunthorpe some of its local rock, sandstone, and Nunthorpe's sample offered an INSET opportunity – the class teacher wrote: 'Around Nunthorpe the soil is heavy clay, but there is a dispute among the staff as to whether the rock is glacial, sandstone or iron ore (to name but a few). I am trying to contact the local Heritage Centre where they have a display of local geology, but their phone is on fax mode!'

The Land Use – UK survey was an integral part of a contrasting UK locality study in both schools. As part of this cross-curricular topic with a geographical focus, the children exchanged work on bus timetables, book reviews, aerial photographs and landscape paintings before they took part in the survey.

Parents and members of the local community helped Harthill pupils survey their square. They finished off with a picnic in the school grounds and an animated discussion about the speed of cars on the road outside school, which they decided was the main environmental issue in their square. The midday assistant explained to the children that the field she farmed opposite school was 'setaside'. She had tried a succession of crops and all had been eaten by badgers and rabbits. 'It was prudent to leave the land and be paid to do so', she said. Nunthorpe had not had any 'setaside' in their square. They were interested in Harthill's explanation. Sophisticated concepts can be introduced because they are made immediate, relevant and personal by way of twinning.

The Nunthorpe square provided a number of contrasts and helped Harthill children appreciate what it was like to live in a suburban environment. The two schools served very different areas, but both schools mentioned traffic as a problem, and a common desire to cut pollution was evident. Nunthorpe thought that in 20 years' time the fields around their school would be developed for housing, but Harthill foresaw few changes in housing; the subsequent discussion led to a greater understanding of the factors which influence the location of housing development. Both schools buried a time-capsule, including letters to children who would be at the schools, to be opened in the year 2020.

Harthill and Foula

Foula Primary in Shetland was also twinned with Harthill. The Foula children sent descriptions of their locality to Harthill: 'not very many people', 'not polluted', 'lots of boats', 'no football pitches'; and they made a list of questions to ask the Harthill children. After Harthill had read the information sent them, Tim said he was 'surprised they've even got a Post Office'. Elouise remarked 'I think they'd have to learn to spin wool and fish like their parents.' They were surprised that e-mail and fax machines were used regularly by Foula school. Stereotypical views of people and places are less likely to form when information about real people is exchanged in this way.

The Foula square was the highest place on the island, and the children there thought it was exposed. Like Harthill they didn't want their square to change much, and thought it would be exactly the same in 20 years' time – heathland, bog and loch – although they did think that there would be more birds breeding there in the future. Harthill have asked them why, and what birds are there at present.

Information received by Harthill from both Nunthorpe and Foula was put on a database, and the children have handled and interpreted this data. Now that the children in each locality are familiar with the land-use survey categories, it is intended that each will survey another 1km square adjacent to the original one surveyed. An ongoing mapmaking process in each location!

Winchester and Liverpool

King Alfred's College of Higher Education, Winchester, and Liverpool Hope University College exchanged maps, data and photographs of locations covered by their student surveyors. The basic techniques in the Land Use – UK survey were examined and compared with other methodologies in land-use mapping as part of the students' coursework in their geography studies. BEd and PGCE students training to be primary teachers appreciated the opportunity for a meaningful study of contrasting localities through the twinning process.

Kyle and Aylesbury

Kyle Academy in Ayr surveyed four squares some distance apart. Using the principal teacher of geography's Volvo for transport, the sixth-form class of five students were 'press-ganged' into service. The group covered three hundred miles in three days; the furthest square was completed by the teacher, David Eddon, himself.

As Scottish schools break up for the summer holiday two weeks before their English counterparts, David decided to pay a visit to Kyle's twinned school, Aylesbury High in Buckinghamshire. Kyle Academy is co-educational, whereas Aylesbury High is a girls' school, and significantly larger. David reported a most enjoyable and interesting visit, including a conducted tour by Year-9 pupils. Subsequently Aylesbury High received a bumper packet of Land Use – UK and Kyle Academy information which was used in the display in their school to mark Geography Action Week.

Jane Brownlee, Head of Geography at Aylesbury High, explained an activity which took place in Action Week in a letter to her colleague in Ayr:

> Today our Year-12 geographers, who did not take part in the survey, have had a field trip to Ayr, Kilmarnock, and your three rural squares. We compared and contrasted 'views and visions', a most useful and fascinating exercise. We do appreciate the generous donation of maps and photographs. If you need maps of this area for a display any time, do let us know.

Three of the Year-12 Aylesbury students wrote about their impressions of Scotland after their field trip:

> I originally thought Scotland was a country of open hilly moorlands and not many residential areas. The information given to us by Kyle Academy confirmed some of my views but made me more aware of the close proximity of the forest to the surrounding towns.
>
> I didn't realise that there were so many variations in land use in Scotland and that there were forests so close to towns.
>
> It was interesting to see the differences in land use in a relatively small area of Scotland.

Kyle students employed the following descriptions to describe their squares: all coniferous forest; pastoral farmland; residential; and open hilly moorland. Among the issues they raised were: the possible health risks associated with pylons; forestry development impinging on previously open hilly moorland; limited access in the coniferous forest; and noise pollution caused by heavy traffic. This variety provided rich material for comment and discussion for their Aylesbury 'twins'.

Both schools intend to use their link to focus study of a contrasting region in Britain. Year-8 students are exchanging weather data; Year 9 will exchange information on the landscape, the use of lochs, and weathering; Year 11 will exchange agricultural and industrial topics; and Year 12 (who intend to converse on the Internet) will exchange information on County Structure Plans and development.

As in other Land Use – UK twinning partnerships, students will have the opportunity to observe closely changes affecting the lives of the inhabitants of their twinned locality, as they occur. Colleagues working together in this way not only make their geography lessons more real and interesting, they also provide positive professional support and co-operation in these times of much educational change.

Chester and Sidcup

Overleigh St Mary's C of E Primary School in Chester was twinned with Royal Park Primary School, Sidcup, Kent. Initial perceptions of Sidcup were recorded by Chester children before they had located Sidcup in an atlas:

> Sidcup is down south, near London somewhere.
>
> My granddad used to live in London and now he lives in Kent and so I think it's a place with lots of bungalows.
>
> Sidcup probably has lots of houses for people who work in London.
>
> It might have part of the River Thames going through.

Recording the children's initial perceptions in their own words is important: comparisons between their initial perceptions and informed judgements provides tangible evidence of learning and development and forms an excellent basis for assessment. When the Chester children received the data from Sidcup, they appreciated that the square only represented a small area but were very keen to investigate it. They were surprised at the extent of farmland, but quickly realised that the square was at the edge of the district. They were pleased to find that the evidence supported some of their initial views – examination of the map confirmed that a tributary of the Thames and a railway line to London ran through the square.

Chester is a tourist city, and the Overleigh children's comments and views on their own square tended to reflect this. During the course of completing their own survey, they had waved at and spoken to numerous visitors who were curious to know what they were doing. They looked at the changes that the Sidcup children wanted to see in their square (e.g. a special area in the 'meadows' where children can play freely close to the river and paddle safely) and considered themselves lucky that they already had this in The Meadows area of Handbridge, Chester.

Malpas and Llanwrda

Another insight the children have derived from Land Use – UK is a better appreciation of the differences in language and culture that exist within the UK. Children at Malpas Alport Endowed Primary School, Cheshire, twinned with Ysgol Caio in Llanwrda, Carmarthen, were impressed that the Welsh children were bilingual before they went to high school, and would themselves like to learn another language. They conducted a survey on a preferred second language. Most chose French: Welsh, Chinese and German collected only two votes each!

The Malpas children used the Llanwrda Land Use – UK data and accompanying letters to compare local dairy farming with the sheep farms in Llanwrda. They also compared the human influences in both locations: very few cars in Llanwrda, but traffic congestion in Malpas. Only one Malpas child wanted to live in Llanwrda, however; the others preferred to put up with noise pollution in order to have more amenities and be close to friends.

Malpas children thought that there would be plenty of fresh air with no pollution in Llanwrda and that it would be a peaceful place to live. They compiled a list of questions to ask:

- How do you organise friends to play?
- What language do you speak at home?
- When did your village shop close?
- What do you like and dislike about living in Llanwrda?
- Where do your parents work?
- Where do you shop?

Malpas children compared the 'national issues' form, Task 2 of the survey, for both locations. Only two houses had been built in Llanwrda during the last five years, whereas forty houses are currently being built in and around Malpas. They discussed the consequences of more houses being built – two of which were 'more children to play with' and 'larger classes in school'. They estimated that there were 750–1000 houses in Malpas compared with only 30 in Llanwrda and looked at the reasons why more people lived in Malpas.

This work forms an excellent basis for understanding the hierarchy of settlement. Some information was provided by adults, but the primary source for their views of their twinned locality was information provided by the children who live there. This leads to an appreciation of how the size of places, and the services available, have an impact on children's lives. In addition, giving recognition and credence to young children's views about the environment increases their sense of involvement and pride in their own 'place'.

In summary

The two sets of data and the work which resulted from the comparison formed the basis of exciting and informative displays in many school entrance halls and geography departments. The benefits of the twinning experience are evident regardless of the age of the surveyors – infants and undergraduates alike have shared survey information about their twinned localities with their local communities.

Communication skills have been developed by the exercise, and students are also much more aware of similarities and differences in land use between different parts of the UK. They have begun to appreciate the variety of cultures, educational systems – even languages – within the kingdom, and how these factors affect real people in real places.

Many of the twinning partnerships are at an early stage, but some groups have gone beyond exchanging data and have begun to develop successful curriculum initiatives, and many more have material ready to develop links in the future. There is evidence to suggest that twinning has not been confined to the schools and groups linked by the Geographical Association: some schools are now exchanging land-use data within their own city or county to point up contrasts in a more local context. Some links, no doubt, will only endure for a short time, specifically in connection with Land Use – UK; others may continue. It will be interesting to see how concern about the local environment is maintained by the participants, and whether the hopeful 'visions' of the future offered by the children will be realised in the new millennium in which they will grow up.

Some benefits accruing from the twinning experience:

- It fulfils the National Curriculum requirement to study a contrasting locality.

- Awareness of outside interest heightens children's civic pride and self-esteem.

- It uses primary sources to develop data-handling and analysis skills.

- It helps children develop a resistance to stereotypical views.

- A comparison of the children's initial perceptions with their informed judgements provides evidence of progression and a basis for assessment.

Chapter 11:
To Scotland and suburbia

Frances Francis and Paula Richardson

The two accounts which follow illustrate the vast range of pleasures and problems encountered by the surveyors. The first is from a Head of Geography at a small girls' school near London; the second from a Task Force volunteer, 'mopping up' some unallocated key squares in the Scottish highlands.

Photo: Frances Francis

A suburban survey
Frances Francis

Perhaps it *was* a little ambitious to volunteer to survey a kilometre square for Land Use – UK. It seemed such a good idea at the time, and I sent the form in full of enthusiasm. When we learned that we had been allocated a key square, the euphoria lasted until I attempted to work out which square we had been given. Braeside School for Girls is a small private school on the edge of Greater London, and I had asked for a square which was 'local and, if possible, within walking range of the school, as we have no transport.' My first attempt located our square on the south coast! I am still in the dark ages of letters and numbers, but fortunately my husband is familiar with the new way of locating grid squares: my despair turned to joy when I discovered that not only was the square very local but also centred on my house, so we could use that as a base for our survey.

After receiving the official pack I had to decide how to tackle the project, and which pupils should do it. I realised that at least two days would be needed – preferably in a block so that the analysis could be done immediately afterwards. As luck would have it the senior girls were going to France for two days, so we had to devise some activities for the middle school: a small but lively group of Year 7s became my survey team.

Next step was to sort out a field map. Not as easy as it sounds: the OS 1:10 000 map of our square is dated 1986, since when a lot of development has taken place. A large development on an old hospital site looked as though it might repay investigation, so we took a Sunday afternoon stroll to the site. Jackpot: a site plan complete with street names. My husband enlarged the 1:10 000 map to 1:5 000 and reduced the site plan to approximately 1:5 000 so that we could cut and paste onto our new base map and draw in other new roads. I created a key of the survey categories and made field maps that fitted onto an A4 sheet. (Thank goodness for the OS photocopy licence!)

In between setting and marking exams, writing reports and preparing Year 9s for their Duke of Edinburgh Award expeditions, I managed to send out a permission letter to parents and put together field packs for the staff and instruction sheets for the girls. All I had to do now was somehow find time to explain it all to the girls and give them health and safety guidance. We contacted the local newspaper, who put a few paragraphs in one edition and promised to photograph the girls on the day. The excitement was enormous.

I begged a couple of extra lessons with my group to prepare for the survey. We went over the categories, how and what to mark on the map, things to look out for in order to complete Tasks 2 and 3, and what to photograph. I split the girls into three groups, allocating to each group one-third of the square and an adult helper. I explained how to do the fieldwork and issued rules about behaviour and safety.

The great day dawned, and panic set in. Why was I doing this? What on earth made me think we could survey accurately a whole square kilometre in one day? Where were the badges? On my desk at school, and the girls due to arrive at 8.30! Enter one life-saver son, who drove me to school and back. What would I do without my family? How do other geography teachers cope?

Suddenly the day was under way. Each group set off with instructions to be back for lunch at 12.30. My group asked questions, wrote notes, took photographs, and were amazed at what they found out about the area. They got hooked on the history of Harts House, now converted to a nursing home, whose grounds are the building-site mentioned earlier. They 'discovered' the old village pump and the butcher's shop – preserved by his widow exactly as it was the day her husband died. I knew some local history, but the girls' enthusiasm opened my eyes to things I had taken for granted.

Back home for lunch, we compared notes with the other groups. One group had done their area very quickly, but the other still had half their allocated area to cover. I gave the group who had finished some of the second group's work. My own group also had a large area still to complete. Much to my relief the photographer arrived at 1.30. We set out with instructions to meet again at 3.30.

I had thought the field day was going to be the hardest, and it was certainly exhausting. I said goodbye to the last girl at 4.00, put my feet up and opened the local paper. Disaster – there was a picture of the Year 10s and 12s at our local girls' grammar school looking at the area they were surveying for Land Use – UK. Would all our hard work be eclipsed by the older girls? After a cup of tea I began to think it was not such a disaster. We could swap results, have a combined display or at least co-operate over where the display could go. In the meantime, we still had day two to tackle.

Friday dawned and we had the whole day, and the whole school, to ourselves in which to complete the colouring in and analysis. How naive can one be! I had forgotten how long children take to colour in maps, especially when there is only one set of the right colours available. We struggled on, but came to a grinding halt when I realised that my 'fast' group had not recorded one area accurately, so I popped out at lunch to have another look. We also had several queries about colouring in. Through GA headquarters I was able to contact Mike Morrish, who sorted out our problems, so it was full steam ahead once again.

We discussed the issues for Task 2 and agreed on what we would write on the reporting sheet for Task 3. For Task 2 the loss of local shops was a major issue. We decided this was due in part to parking problems in the older shopping areas, and – because most residents have a car – competition from large supermarkets outside the area. For Task 3 the girls summed the area up as: 'an attractive, affluent, suburban residential area mainly developed in the 1920s and 1930s'. Their view of the future is depressing: unless development is controlled they foresee even more infill housing, no gardens and even more traffic on bigger and busier roads. And we are officially a conservation area. What hope do other areas have?

We completed the task and sent off the results; I hope our efforts are accurate enough. Now it is over I am glad we took the plunge. The girls worked very hard and experienced a great sense of achievement, especially when their photograph appeared in the local paper. I know they got immense satisfaction out of doing the survey and were very proud to take part.

Photo: Paula Richardson

Voyage of discovery: Stuart pilots the borrowed boat

A force to be reckoned with

Paula Richardson

We reconcile ourselves to the occasional drudgery of existence by promising ourselves 'One day, we will ...' – but usually we never do. Volunteering for the Land Use – UK Task Force gave me and two other Sassenach geographers the chance to fulfil at least one promise we made ourselves years ago, namely to visit the Highlands of Scotland. We hadn't reckoned on the Task Force Co-ordinator supporting our project *quite* so enthusiastically – we were a little taken aback when he gave us twenty squares to do!

We travelled in a Peugeot 106: Val Banks, Stuart May and I, plus luggage, clipboards, maps (carefully prepared by Stuart), and of course the packet of crayons. Little did we know that most of the crayons would never be needed, while 'laser lemon' and 'green' were worn down to mere stubs ...

We set ourselves a target of two squares a day, and banished from our minds all thought of mists coming down suddenly on large tracts of uninhabited featureless terrain. Our bed-and-breakfast landladies were very impressed to be hosting land-use surveyors and heaped extra bacon on our breakfast plates 'to keep out the cold on the tops'.

Our first two squares were near Applecross on the west coast, then we crossed to Skye for two more squares. This gave us the chance to use the new Skye bridge, and we were curious to know how the locals felt about this rather controversial construction. There seemed to be a general feeling that Skye had been deprived of its island status and that the nature of the islanders' lives had changed for ever. Toll costs, levied on lorries and buses as well as cars, were reflected in the higher price of goods on the island; we noticed particularly the increased price of the cream teas we consumed as we travelled around in the course of our duties.

The people we met were usually very helpful and often very interested in what we were doing. On one occasion an estate manager was persuaded to let us use his small motorboat to take us four miles up a loch, thereby saving hours of walking and giving us a very pleasant experience into the bargain. Gillies and estate managers kindly let us drive along private roads to the start points for our climbs. Our small car proved very manoeuvrable in these conditions, performing three-point turns in narrow tracks with ease: we all feel quite equal to a major rally round Scotland.

The distances between our far-flung squares meant that time off for sightseeing was limited. However, we did manage to visit Plockton, near the Kyle of Lochalsh; a very pretty coastal village with palm trees flourishing in the Gulf Stream climate. Uncanny, we thought, no television aerials; then we stumbled across large outside-broadcast vans and film crews in the narrow lanes. We were pleased not to have to find a category for TV film-making.

We travelled north as far as Ullapool, then turned east and south. Here we came across one of our greatest challenges – a square dedicated to the cultivation of row upon row of 25-year-old conifers, stretching into the distance as far as the eye could see. After an hour of wandering about looking for a possible lake in the centre of the plantation, it dawned on us that we didn't know where we were: even our compass had lost heart in the face of so much greenery. Then suddenly it was five pm, and nowhere else on earth does this hour have quite the same significance as in Scotland: it is the signal to every midge for hundreds of miles to home in on human flesh, reducing strong men and women to gibbering wrecks. A low point.

Perhaps the most controversial phenomenon we witnessed during our visit was the large-scale development of Scottish estates for leisure use. The 'big house' and other estate properties are now rented out for house parties at thousands of pounds a week; wealthy people fly in from abroad to hunt, shoot and fish. While this provides some employment for local people, we also found evidence that long-standing tenants had been evicted from estate houses to provide more accommodation for short-term visitors. This type of change is bound to alter the Highlands for ever; the landscape is well-maintained, grouse are encouraged and deer numbers controlled, but traditional ways of farming and small communities – already barely viable – are seriously at risk.

Out of the 'random' selection of squares we did seem to have been allocated a disproportionately large number of high, open, bleak moorland landscapes. The concept of 'heathland and bog' is now firmly fixed in our minds! One of our major challenges was knowing – after walking and climbing in such terrain for two hours or more without GPS equipment – when we were 'there'. The beauty of a team of three is that one can lie, two can agree to lie, but three makes for honesty! We thought that it would be easier to locate ourselves in a landscape with trees and peaks, rather than open moorland with a scattering of stones, but this was not always so. It was strange, too, how often on the ground different lakes looked the same shape, with the same features around them: occasionally we felt as though we had wandered into *Alice in Wonderland*. And while we had all, at some time in our teaching careers, trotted out those old maxims about fieldwork, we were shocked to find that these were often true – for instance:

- Sheep tracks *are* better defined than footpaths.
- Footpaths inevitably end in someone's back garden.
- All that shines green on a mountain is not grass.
- Distances on the map bear no relationship to those on the ground.
- If the contours on a map are close together it really *is* steep!

However, we let nothing detract from our pleasure at being there: the view from the tops was always glorious, and as geographers we revelled in the fresh air, the striking landscape and the wonderful weather. (It also made a refreshing change not to be encumbered with a gaggle of children demanding to know when it was lunchtime!) The joy of this project was that it gave us a reason to visit the Highlands; we were doubly rewarded by the sense of achievement we experienced – not only in finding and surveying the correct squares, but in making a significant contribution to Land Use – UK.

*The Director of
Education in Cheshire
with three young
Cheshire surveyors*

Chapter 12:
Using Land Use – UK for a county-wide initiative

Jeremy Krause

Land Use – UK has provided many interesting and innovative educational opportunities. Most important of all has been the opportunity to engage in an activity with clear guidelines which has allowed the County's schools to develop a broad view of Cheshire in the Britain of 1996. It has also sparked off fresh GA branch activity county-wide.

We are using the results in many ways:

- To provide an archive for future generations: this will be deposited in the Cheshire Record Office.
- To provide a database for existing land-use surveyors: to help them observe, monitor and record changes in their county.
- To encourage further land-use survey work within the county, both in the short and long term. A good example is that of Tarporley High School, which is co-operating with Kelsall Primary and other feeder schools to use Land Use – UK to support key stage 2/3 cross-phase work. The intention is that new Year-7 children will bring their schools' land-use squares with them to compare with others in the high school's catchment area. This will give added status to the geographical investigations undertaken in the primary phase.
- To provide a focal point for the re-establishment of Geographical Association branch activities in Cheshire: in the recent past Cheshire has had two GA branches – Chester, and Crewe and Nantwich – but for various reasons both of them had ceased to operate. Now Land Use – UK has provided a focus for reviving branch activity.
- To help schools to place their locality studies within a wider geographical framework: the National Curriculum Orders for Geography contain requirements at key stages 1, 2 and 3 for the investigations of place to be put into a wider geographical context. There is also a requirement at key stages 2 and 3 to investigate the geographical themes at local, regional and national scale. Land Use – UK gives children of all ages good opportunities to do this.

What went on?

'Share a Square in Cheshire' day

This was held during Geography Action Week, and consisted of exhibitions and presentations of the results from more than fifty of the Cheshire survey groups. The results provided a fascinating perspective on the concerns of Cheshire children and adults in 1996. During the afternoon a huge map of Cheshire was created on the floor of the hall and colour copies of the 1:5 000-scale maps were positioned on it by those whose conducted the survey.

'Share a Square' day was attended by over 120 children, teachers, governors and members of the public.

Exhibitions around Cheshire

Some of the displays from 'Share a Square' day were exhibited at County Hall during November 1996 where they demonstrated the exciting work in which the county's young geographers have been engaged. They attracted a great deal of interest, and during coming months the displays will be shown at other events such as the county's Education Show in February, as well as being available for schools to use.

Publishing the Cheshire results

We plan to publish the results as a CD-ROM: this will allow the land-use squares to be compared visually, and will also enable us to provide supporting information, including:

- A 1:5 000-scale map of each of the squares, provided by the Cheshire County Council's Geographic Information Unit.
- Photographs of a representative set of land uses from across the county and from each square.
- Video footage giving the 'views and visions' from eight groups representing the eight Cheshire districts. It is intended to combine these with the photographic and map evidence.
- Brief written summaries of each square. These will incorporate key words for use in a word-search routine which will support the investigation of the similarities and differences between squares. The list of key words and a response from a typical school are given below.
- Statistical analyses of the data. The Cheshire results will be used in a variety of comparative studies.
- Other related data from the County Council: this includes aerial photographs from the 1970s, 1980s and 1990s, as well as material relating to Cheshire's environmental measures relating to wildlife, transport, energy, water, waste disposal and land use.

The written summaries

For inclusion on the CD, schools are asked to write between 200 and 300 words about each square. They are also expected to check the list of key words in the panel, using those which are suitable and suggesting additions.

Key words

arable, canals, churches, commuters, corner shops, cows, dairy, derelict, farms, flat, flats, gardens, golf course, grass, hilly, horses, houses, hypermarkets, industry, land in transition, loam, medical services, motorways, new, new houses, offices, old, parks, playgrounds, playing fields, public offices, pylons, quarries, railways, roads, rural, sand, schools, setaside, sheep, shops, suburbs, town centre, undulating, urban, utilities, village, water, woods.

A typical response: a school's report on the village of Sound

We live in rural countryside. There are a lot of farms around Sound. There is also a lot of grass for the animals to eat. There are dairy farms and many horses. You will see a lot of cows and bulls and you have to be careful of the brine pit in the fields and the ponds. There are tractors and when we did the walk they were baling. It was haymaking time.

There are a few woods around Sound. We do not have many houses, the only playing field and playground are at our school. There is only one school, ours. All the houses have gardens, many people have large gardens and fields. There is one very busy main road that runs through the centre of the village, it has lots of small lanes off it. We have no shops, offices or factories, in fact there is no centre to the village.

Nicola Millard (Year 5) and Nicola Barbour (Year 6),
pupils at Sound County Primary School, near Nantwich, Cheshire

Teaching and learning geography

The advice to all Cheshire schools when they construct their teaching schemes for geography is to use the enquiry approach. It is also important to show them how they can link the Land Use – UK data fully into their schemes of work so that it becomes integral to the curriculum. To ensure that the same message goes out with all publications and INSET, the basic questions in the panel on the right are used to structure the children's investigation of places and environments. They are based on an article by Michael Storm in *Primary Geographer* (1989).

Conclusion

In Cheshire, Land Use – UK came at a very timely moment. The county is about to be reorganised under local government review, and geography is becoming well embedded into the school curriculum. The time is right for the rejuvenation of GA branch activities, and the focus is being placed by all of us on the nature of the county and the country in the new millennium.

There is no shortage of issues for Cheshire's geographers to address!

1 What is the square like?
Locating:
Where is the square within Cheshire, the North-West and the UK?

Comparing:
How is this square's land use similar to that of another square? Or how is it different?

2 Why is the land used as it is?
Analysing:
What activities are there in the area?
Why are they here?
How are they organised?

3 How is this square connected to other places?
Developing geographical awareness:
What are the transport, political and other connections between this square and other squares in Cheshire, North-West England, the UK, Europe and the rest of the world?

4 How is this square changing?
Developing understanding:
In what ways is this area changing, and why?
Who is being affected by these changes most/least?

5 What does it feel like to be in this square?
(This links well with the 'views and visions' aspect of the survey.)
Developing values and attitudes:
What are the similarities and differences between this square and other squares?
Has someone else whom you know been to your square?
What did he/she like best/least?

Photo: Tony Stone/Trevor Wood

Chapter 13:
Sheet 77 revisited –
a diary of events

Tony Binns

11 April 1996: GA Annual Conference at Southampton. A constant buzz of activity around the Land Use – UK exhibit; the large map of allocated squares is filling up with coloured dots as more and more schools sign up to take part. As I pause to look I am nabbed by Rex Walford: 'Tony, how about getting the Brighton branch to re-survey Sheet 77 of the Second Land Utilisation Survey? We are keen to have one or two entire sheets re-surveyed as part of the Land Use – UK project.' What can I say, except that it seems an excellent thing to do. (I haven't actually seen Sheet 77 so can't tell what I'm getting into here ...)

15 April: Unearth Sheet 77 in the University Map Library. It covers 200 square kilometres of the Sussex coast centred on Brighton and Hove, extending westwards to Shoreham harbour, Shoreham-by-Sea and the Adur valley and eastwards to Saltdean and Telscombe Cliffs. The southern third of the sheet is water – the English Channel. To the north, the built-up area extends up a number of dry valleys in the South Downs, following the main transport routes to London and Lewes, and including residential estates such as Woodingdean and Bevendean to the east of Brighton, and Mile Oak to the north and west of Hove. It is an area of considerable beauty and sharp contrasts. It is also quite large.

Discuss the idea with colleagues Jon May and Simon Rycroft, and they agree it is a worthwhile project. Jon and I will raise the matter at the next branch meeting.

15 May: Committee meeting: about a dozen members gather. When we reach 'Any other business' I unfurl Sheet 77 on the lounge carpet and ask those present if they would be willing to embark on the re-surveying of the sheet. There is a prolonged silence ... broken by Alan Grey, our longstanding branch treasurer and Head of Geography at Varndean Sixth Form College, who remarks that in the 1960s the sheet had been surveyed by pupils from his school, when it was Varndean Grammar School. This breaks the ice, and other committee members join in: 'Do you mean the whole thing?' – 'I can't possibly see how I can fit it in on top of everything else'. Then the mood becomes more positive. 'We would kick ourselves afterwards if we don't', says one; another comments: 'This is an historic once-and-for-all opportunity.' Am cautiously optimistic.

16 May: Phone Rex to ask him to come down to Sussex to explain the project and to animate and enthuse my prospective surveyors. It needs to be soon: finding a date is difficult, but Rex decides that if he leaves the RGS Council meeting early he can come to Brighton on 10 June. I book a lecture theatre at the University and mobilise our branch 'telephone tree'.

10 June: Our meeting with Rex. There are twelve teachers, representing ten schools, plus my colleague Jon May and the University Map Curator, Jonathan Rowell, who has agreed to copy and advise on the maps we shall need. I chair the meeting. Rex outlines the Land Use – UK project and its historical context – the two national land-use surveys directed by Dudley Stamp in the 1930s and Alice Coleman in the 1960s. As ever, Rex charms everyone with his effervescence and enthusiasm, and soon we all share his fervent desire to have Sheet 77 re-surveyed. Questions are raised about practicalities, and we agree that teachers should do a reconnaissance of the area before going out with their students, and that new features, such as a recent bypass, must be added to the printed maps. There are still concerns about the time-consuming nature of this huge project, but we decide to press ahead. Will try to allocate more squares to branch members over the next few weeks.

12 June: Ask Jon Rowell for two enlarged copies of each of the squares on Sheet 77 for use by our surveyors. Discuss the project with Jon May and Simon Rycroft again; we recognise that branch members may not be able to complete the task on their own and that we should have a contingency plan. Our freshers will be having an induction and orientation weekend on 19–20 October, and we could mobilise over 100 students in the field. We decide to set aside the whole of Saturday 19 October to complete as many squares as possible.

The summer passes. Branch members have gone their separate ways. I tackle a square myself: it takes about a day to complete. I wonder how many squares we will have covered by the time we meet again ...

10 September: Branch committee meeting. We discover we have completed 39 of the 138 squares: clearly, there is still much work to be done. An enterprising committee member has bought, on behalf of the branch, 20 copies of Sheet 77 from Alice Coleman and now distributes them.

9 October: After the inaugural lecture of the branch winter programme, the committee has another urgent discussion. We have surveyed less than a third of the squares, and everything now depends on how many squares the first-year undergraduates can survey later in the month. Simon Rycroft promises to help plan the complex logistical exercise of getting 108 students to and from their survey locations on the day.

14 October: Today, Simon and I should have met to plan the field-day, but he is not in. I later learn that he has suspected malaria, probably contracted during our geography field course in The Gambia last year.

16 October: Our fears are realised: blood tests confirm that Simon does have malaria and will be out of action for several weeks. Jon May kindly agrees to step in, and helps me to allocate squares to pairs of students. Jon Rowell helps with the photocopying of maps, and we devise a set of instructions for students and drivers on each of the nine minibus routes which will take students to and from their survey locations.

Each minibus can hold six pairs of students, making a total of 54 pairs, each with the maps of one or two kilometre grid squares which they are being asked to cover. Each driver will be given a 1:25 000 map to show the location of the survey squares in a broader context and to indicate the best access points. We are hiring only six

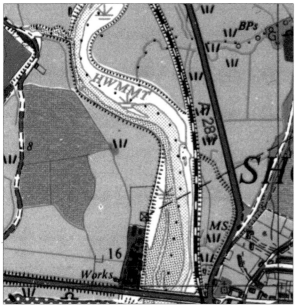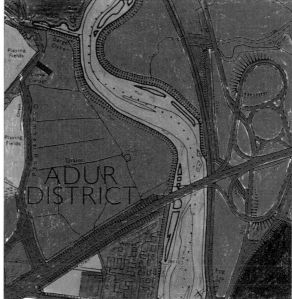

vehicles, so three drivers must do two routes. Montgomery of Alamein would have been impressed with our battle-plan!

19 October: Mercifully, it is bright, sunny and mild – the last weekend of British Summer Time. Six of us meet up at the University at 7.45 am to travel to Crawley to collect the hired minibuses. This takes longer than expected but we are back for the briefing at 9.30 am.

Jon May introduces the briefing, examining the history of land-use surveys and considering such issues as citizenship and the political message inherent in Dudley Stamp's choice of colours for the maps of the First Land Utilisation Survey. I then explain various logistical matters and ask the students to line up in pairs – mixed where possible, though two-thirds of our first-year students are female. The line stretches from the lecture theatre along the corridor and through the fire doors to the Map Library, where I give each pair their group number and minibus allocation and hand them two copies of the grid square maps they are to survey. As only a few students are familiar with the area, I have also prepared for each pair a section from the 1:25 000 sheet showing the general location of their square. As the end of the line approaches, it becomes apparent that some students have been too shy to find a partner; I engage in some impromptu 'social engineering'.

A young lady wearing a large hat and long skirt returns to say that she has somehow missed her minibus. As I try to resolve the problem it is also disturbingly apparent that she is not wearing shoes – how will she cope with the fieldwork? Presumably erstwhile pop-singer Sandie Shaw managed to cope with such challenges! Another arrives late and bleary-eyed, claiming that she has overslept; I remember that she apologised earlier that week for missing a lecture, also due to 'oversleeping'. Fortunately, her square is the one in which the university is based, but she is not pleased to receive this information, exclaiming indignantly 'I could have stayed in bed an hour longer!'

The students are swiftly and smoothly dispatched, but it seems no time at all before we have to rendezvous with them and bring them back to the university. In between I manage a short meeting with colleagues to discuss the aims and conduct of the seminars we are to lead later in the afternoon.

Part of Sheet 77 of the Second Land Utilisation Survey (left), with the same area as re-surveyed in 1996 (right). According to the legend, the area was surveyed in 1965–67 'by G. A. Sinclair, C. Watson BA, P. H. Richards, J. D. Turner MA and pupils of Varndean Grammar School'. In 1996, the surveyors were members of the Brighton Branch of the Geographical Association and first-year undergraduates of the University of Sussex Based upon the Ordnance Survey map with the permission of the Controller of Her Majesty's Stationery Office © Crown copyright

Photo: Michael Howarth

Tony demonstrating the scale of the project he had undertaken at the launch of the Land Use - UK results at the RGS

Feedback discussion goes surprisingly well and I am impressed with the level of interest shown and the relatively few problems experienced by students in the field. There were, however, one or two exceptions. One pair of students describe how they had to climb barbed-wire fences (!) on a farm to gain access to a vantage point overlooking their area. Apparently at one point they spotted a farmer and heard a gun being fired ... Other challenges were less life-threatening: differentiating between tended open space and grassland, and wondering how to categorise allotments. For most the exercise went smoothly – as one student observed, 'Our biggest problem was finding somewhere to stop for lunch.'

After considering the mechanics of the exercise, the seminar moves on to discuss broader issues such as whether the survey would promote citizenship and who should 'own' the data.

25 October: I look through the maps coloured by the students (using the specified sets of crayons, efficiently provided at short notice by Julia Legg from GA headquarters). Students have also written up their experiences and thoughts in a 1000-word 'critical analysis' of the project as a whole and of their own particular grid-square survey.

The results are impressive. Some students have taken the trouble to support their own critique with detail from the various journal articles we have recommended them to read. One comments: 'I think it is a worthwhile experience and a privilege to take part in a national project like this.' Another writes: 'Geography out of a book is no substitute for "hands-on" experience. That is what was so good about taking part in the Sheet 77 survey – it was real.' Another comments: 'The survey offered an opportunity to learn and/or practise valuable fieldwork skills, which cannot be done in a classroom setting ... I found both the fieldwork and the later discussions both interesting and quite good fun ...'

Altogether, the students have completed 64 grid squares in a single day. I ask our University cartographer to draw up a base map showing the grid squares on Sheet 77; I mark on it those surveyed by the branch and those surveyed by the students. 35 now remain to be surveyed, mainly in the western half: Hove, Southwick and Shoreham. We must mobilise the branch committee again ...

4 November: Get a twelve-minute slot to speak about our project at the launch of the Land Use – UK results, held at the Royal Geographical Society. Pose for photographs brandishing Sheet 77!

5 November: Before letting off my fireworks, I make duplicates of the remaining 35 squares and send them, together with a copy of the base map, to our Joint Branch Chairs, Claire Donaldson and John Whilde, with a letter begging for their help in persuading colleagues to 'get their boots on' again to complete the survey.

12 November: Geography Action Week. On a visit to Boundstone Community College, I take the opportunity to persuade the enthusiastic Head of Geography, Valerie Narayanaswamy, that it would be very much appreciated if she could survey some more squares.

27 November: Another branch committee meeting, and once again I unfurl Sheet 77; also exhibit the map of surveyed squares. Thankfully, everyone rallies round and John Whilde efficiently negotiates the allocation of squares. One member bargains with another to exchange two rural squares for one urban; another (recently retired from teaching) requests a square next to an out-of-town supermarket so that he can combine shopping with surveying!

12 January 1997: Many members of the branch committee have sent me grid squares surveyed during the Christmas holiday – fortunately, they all managed to get them done before the big snow on New Year's Eve! At our next meeting we must take stock of the results, and decide how to get the map published.

20 January: The first branch committee meeting of the New Year. It appears there are just two of the 138 squares still to be done, in the Shoreham area. Everyone is keen to get the exercise completed, and David Williams and Mark Halliwell agree to survey the last two squares. We have a lengthy discussion about applying for funds to get the sheet published: Liz Williams agrees to follow up a lead from Rex and apply to Southover Manor Trust. I need to check on the master sheet that all the grid squares have now been surveyed and to hand the sheets over to Rex. When I think of the thousands of 'person-hours' involved in the survey, perhaps I should arrange for a police escort when I transport the data to Cambridge!

It has been touch and go, and at times I have felt that we have bitten off more than we can chew. But with the help and commitment of over 100 people, the task is now virtually completed. It has been good for the branch to be involved in such a project – a stimulating variation on the annual routine of lectures and sixth-form conferences. Our first-year students have also profited from their involvement – we might undertake such projects on a regular basis in future. We still have to bring together the data from all 138 grid squares to produce a completed map. But the 1990s map will, we think, be very different from that of the 1960s. It should be a revealing (and satisfying) map to add to our collection.

*Dr Christie Willatts with
members of the First
Land Utilisation Survey
team in their LSE office*

Chapter 14: The changing context of land-use surveys

Simon Rycroft

During the summer of 1996, Jon May, Tony Binns and I monitored the implementation and conduct of Land Use – UK, independently assessing the vision of geography suggested by the exercise[1].

Here, I work through some of the ways in which the 1996 survey is influenced by traditions of land-use mapping in Britain and builds upon them. This is done by exploring two aspects: the first concerns the land-use survey tradition as environmental or geographical education with a powerful and far-reaching role in inculcating sensitive and responsible environmental citizenship. The second follows on from this, and raises a few doubts as to whether the explicit and conscious connections made with that survey tradition in the 1996 Survey Pack and other documentation for Land Use – UK hinders a more progressive and critical role for today's geography.

However, some of my reservations are tempered by other findings on our project presented in Jon May's account (Chapter 15), which stresses that, in emphasising different contexts from those suggested by Land Use – UK in their teaching of the survey, some teachers successfully resurrected land-use survey as a radical and contemporary endeavour. Indeed, when presented with the dry accounts of previous land-use surveys, it is quite difficult to appreciate that, for their time, they were underlain by quite progressive motivations. The second aspect explored here emphasises this point by assessing the ways in which the entwined vision of citizenship and geographical imagination found in the 1930s survey lasted long into the period of post-war reconstruction in Britain.

Education and citizenship: the land–use survey tradition

The Stamp survey

The Land Utilisation Survey of Britain, conducted between 1930 and 1934, and directed by Dudley Stamp, serves as a set piece for geographical and environmental education in the inter- and post-war periods (Stamp 1962; Rycroft and Cosgrove 1994, 1995). It encapsulated an emergent geographical imagination which informed not only environmental consciousness but the consciousness and application of post-war reconstruction policies. Now Land Use – UK reaffirms that land-use surveys of different genres form the central tenet of geographical education to this day. It also characterises a long-standing disciplinary commitment to elucidating human–environment relations in the field.

[1] *This chapter arises from a research project entitled 'Education and Citizenship: Mapping the Land in the 1996 Land Use – UK Survey' funded by the British Academy.*

The Land Utilisation Survey represented the first national land-use survey. It mapped every acre of land in Britain, was directed by Stamp at the London School of Economics and conducted by schoolchildren in the field who were co-ordinated by regional educational organisations. This was not simply for reasons of economy. The work of recording land use was, Stamp felt, a 'magnificent educational exercise involving accurate observation and map reading'. Moreover, since each survey was carried out as part of a national scheme, it 'inculcated an early appreciation of the importance of the unit in a democracy and induced a local pride in achievement'.

For Stamp, then, land-use surveys not only afforded an analysis of how society affected the landscape, but also an important exercise in the education and formation of citizens, in promoting, through fieldwork, a grounded sense of belonging and a responsibility toward the land of Britain. Through the act of mapping, the local could be celebrated and gridded as part of the national, working democratically toward a systematic and efficient use of land. And combining an educational project with a training in citizenship was, Stamp noted, 'basal to any work of national land planning', eventually building a 'better Britain of the future'. This is not to suggest that Stamp anticipated World War II in his project, but that the Depression of the 1930s spawned these Utopian visions; and in many forms Stamp's vision carried over to the period of reconstruction. In this reconstruction, as the 1930–34 land-use surveyors became the planners, they could 'scarcely fail to be thrilled' by the new Britain. Engagement of the young citizen with the land and its functioning, would, Stamp believed, spawn a generation of planners conscious of the complex dialectic operating between the social and the natural worlds.

Using six-inch OS base maps, classes of schoolchildren, directed by their geography teachers in the field, were required to map seven types of land use in their locality, ranging from wasteland to a variety of agricultural and rural uses. The local survey maps were sent to London where Stamp corrected any discrepancies and noted a 'surprising degree of accuracy' as the interests of young people in the land and its problems were aroused. Once calibrated, the data were transposed onto one-inch maps and published in folded and sheet format. Each county's regional survey was recorded in an individual memoir, authored by those with qualifications in geography and with an intimate connection with the locality.

Despite the national coverage and emphasis upon a unified scheme, the uniqueness of the local was also central to the Land Utilisation Survey. As a democratic unit, each county exhibited particular attributes and was located within the national order. Rutland's report, for example, stressed the continuity of land use and independence from many structural changes affecting the nation as a whole, but also the quintessentially English nature of its landscape – an attribute recalled in subsequent disputes surrounding the county's disappearance. It was this notion of variety, or, more precisely, the ecology of variety, which, for Stamp and others during the 1930s, characterised British (especially English) national identity and was ultimately the 'subject' of geography. In textbooks about a variety of (developing) countries, Stamp, often with his wife, was consciously writing of homelands coloured by the perspective of their residents, tempering a concern for the interdependence of environments with a sensitivity to the unique and the particular. This of course is a familiar theme to all teachers of geography today.

Stamp approached geography and geographical education as an holistic study, arguing for the role of the discipline to bridge the gap between the natural and social sciences. Echoing the 'work-place-folk nexus' of earlier regional geographies, the 'unique contribution of the geographer', he felt, was to be a systematic 'holistic approach in which he sees the relationship between man and his environment, with its attendant problems, as a whole'. In this sense, Stamp's version of 'applied geography' worked for the benefit of society, splitting the 'environment' into its component parts and analysing the relative effects of each on 'man'. Ultimately, the geographer provided this complex of data for the purpose of effective physical planning, for 'the application of science in the improvement of the lot of man', as it was put, and through geographical education attempted to 'satisfy the curiosity of men about the world in which they lived', striving to make them 'conscious of their own power to improve their environments'.

In the introduction to *Britain's Structure and Scenery* (1946), a book in the Collins' New Naturalist series, Stamp noted that the wealth of the country's flora and fauna lay in the variety to be found in a small space. Such diversity was directly related to the structure, or geomorphology, of Britain's scenery. The field observers could read the history of the world into their 'homeland' as a 'museum model illustrating the evolution of the world'. Each of the great ages of the Earth's evolution had impacted upon the British Isles, the variety of environments being the 'outward and visible reflection of a long and complex geological history' and the interaction of society. New Naturalists would seek to assess the shifting balance of the ecosystem caused by the interaction of society as it was expressed in land-use changes. Such work would be of the 'highest economic importance ... pregnant with possible scientific results'. This was *not*, then, a conservative endeavour, but prompted the naturalist and geographer to work for collective ecological and economic interests – the two were not necessarily mutually exclusive.

The modern discipline of geography was about systematically mapping this distribution in much of the post-war period, ultimately for social good. To this the ecological metaphor was central and formed the foundation of much of Stamp's self-conscious, albeit scant, theorising on the discipline. In the introduction to his agenda for future study in the new medical geography, *Geography of Life and Death* (1964), for example, he defined ill health and morbidity in terms of lack of harmony between organism and environment, a harmony which could only be realised when society worked consciously with the natural order. Land-use survey was, of course, the best educational exercise to prompt such a realisation.

It was this disconnection between society and nature which was outlined by many in the inter-war period and formed the foundation of the regional survey movement from which the Land Utilisation Survey arose. Stamp adapted the survey scheme, methodology and philosophy of the Land Utilisation Survey from earlier regional surveys inspired by, among others, Patrick Geddes. For accounts of inter-war regional survey work and its contexts, particularly the ways in which it attempted to reconnect the young surveyor with nature for the purpose of encouraging healthy citizenship and sensitive planning, see Matless (1992).

The application of the Land Utilisation Survey was clearly in the realm of national planning. Stamp took the results of the Survey into governmental committees, including the influential Scott committee on rural land-use, of which he was deputy chairman and author of the final report. The Survey depicted vividly the inefficiency of laissez-faire planning – especially the enormous sprawl of urban zones into productive agricultural land. Indeed, perhaps the choice of a colour scheme which was adapted from earlier regional surveys betrays this rural bias. Garish scarlet and purple depicting urban developments was offset by the softer chalky shades of green, brown and yellow representing rural land use. Agriculture was at its lowest point since records had begun, and rural areas were coming under increasing pressure to urbanise – particularly those on the urban fringe. In this, the Survey's underlying concerns reflected a dominant preoccupation of the inter-war period. The aerial perspective offered by the Survey's maps apparently allowed an integrated and holistic appreciation of the ways in which environment and society functioned, or rather malfunctioned. Logically, the ideal aesthetic which the colours of the map and Stamp's writing emphasised was that which married the underlying natural structure of the land – its form – with the pattern of land-use – its function; if form and function harmonised, then so would society and nature.

In short, the Survey and its use captured and directed a particular mid-century understanding of human–environment dialectics, one made vivid by survey in the field. It was also an understanding which was common to many in the post-war planning movement and which informed the logistics and aesthetics of reconstruction. For, in their orderly appearance, new land-use patterns were to reflect a well-ordered democratic society. For Stamp, the planner was an ecological engineer, connecting with and directing the evolution of the surface of the earth. It is impossible to disengage the processes of fieldwork and survey from the conceptualisation of a modernised social and physical order: the good modern citizen had to be educated, and educated geographically.

In the project of post-war reconstruction, then, Stamp's thoughts found resonance. Despite their appearance, modernist developments adopted an approach to human–environment relationships similar to Stamp's, and similarly attempted to match natural order with 'Utopian' social orders. In architectural forms Nature was presented elementally, as a series of harmonious and regular patterns and processes. In the immediate post-war period, then, the educative process of the survey, with its emphasis upon connecting the natural with the social, found renewed importance in the context of social and physical planning. Envisioning humans within a natural order produced a vision of a harmonious environment: from structured molecule, through colloid, cell, organ and individual, to structured society or population, organisation was seen to exist in space and time (see Jellicoe 1960, 1966; Kepes 1956). The project of survey was thus to make clear this innate order.

Within the project of post-war reconstruction, in which he was involved, Stamp's vision of responsible citizenship finds its ultimate expression and we see implicitly the operation of his 'applied geography'. This vision of the modern citizen worked with the common geographical notion that society and the environment must work in harmony to ensure efficient and aesthetically acceptable land-use patterns. Whether we agree with this or not, it is clear that Stamp's Land Utilisation Survey, while a child of its times, did represent a progressive, even radical, project. So, how do other land-use surveys compare?

Re-evaluating reconstruction?

In 1965, the year before Stamp died, a second Land Utilisation Survey was undertaken – directed by Alice Coleman at Kings College, London, and the LSE. The new classifications in this survey reflected prevailing concerns, showing a more technology-inspired attitude toward the environment than the first survey. The techniques for Coleman's survey were similar to Stamp's – mapping on six-inch base maps and employing undergraduates and supervised schoolchildren in the field. But advances in mapping techniques, a change to the scale of the maps produced (1:25 000), and also contemporary concerns, augmented Stamp's 1930s schema. While on the Stamp survey the urban and industrial was depicted in red and purple, more attention was given to the complex patterns of urban land-use in the Coleman survey: OS grey was used to depict residential and commercial uses, and black for derelict land, but both were offset by previously unmapped land-uses such as parks and allotments. Much greater attention was paid to the economic, for example by classifying factories with letter codes and giving transport networks their own colour-coding. Furthermore, other types of land which Stamp's surveyors mapped as unproductive were allocated one of fifteen ecological categories (varieties of meadow grasses, for example). This reflects a growing interest in the environment for its own sake. For the 1960s, the second survey reflected an altered environmental awareness, the growth of modern environmentalism and environmental consciousness. But the survey also represented 'white-heat' technological rhetoric, and seemed not to emphasise the contradiction between the ecological and the industrial: they were considered part of the same wider 'environment'. Nevertheless, there was an emergent tension in this picture which Coleman would build upon in her later research.

Although billed as a land-use survey which would map the changes to the 1930s pattern in the light of upheavals during and after the war, Coleman's survey fed into an ostensibly contrary project. Her work on the failure of modern architecture to accommodate and form healthy citizens in *Utopia on Trial* (1984) perhaps represents what many have called the ecological critique of modernity – that despite the ideals of harmonising nature and humans in a post-war world we were actually further alienated, and that the series of environmental catastrophes of the 1960s were a testament to this. It is interesting to note from the interview with Alice Coleman in Chapter 18 that while she was satisfied with general improvements in agricultural efficiency, the most effective use to which the maps were put was in the field of planning, where she noted surprisingly few improvements. Perhaps the greatest difference between the conduct and underlying concerns of the first and second Land Utilisation Surveys is that the former appears to have been a much more radical and progressive endeavour.

Coleman used computer technology to process her data and was able to devise complex land-use categories. While for reasons of finance few of the second survey's maps were published, the results were published in the standard static manner, freezing the dynamic and multifarious processes which underlay the resultant land-use pattern.

The ITE land cover map

Recently, both Land Utilisation Surveys have been eclipsed by the production of a national land cover map based on satellite images. This was conducted by the Institute of Terrestrial Ecology (ITE) and builds upon the ethos of Stamp's survey, emphasising a lack of any 'ulterior motive' (see Fuller, Sheail and Barr 1994). The new survey takes advantage of advanced digital technology, affording flexibility in scale, projection and information displayed, and is intended for use in environmental, ecological and landscape planning. This survey is therefore as suitable to an age of flexibility as Stamp's was to an age of Modernist planning and development.

While the new land cover map seems to jettison any direct geographical education through field survey, there is an underlying concept of contemporary environmental consciousness, one more sensitised to delicate ecosystemic balances. Once again, it is environmental concern and responsibility which forms the ideological context of land-use (or in this case land-cover) survey. Land-use survey has been central to the foundations of geography, and an important purpose of such surveys has been the identification of people with the land (or nature) and in the process forming good local and national citizens. But the scope of the geographical imagination that such surveys capture and help form is broader than the narrowly defined concerns of geography as a discipline – it finds its way into a more generalised environmental education, and shapes planning and the social order.

Geography and citizenship in Land Use – UK

Having briefly explored the British land-use survey tradition, I want now to express some of my reservations as to the appropriateness of Land Use – UK for contemporary geography. Before I launch into this critique, however, it must be noted that, having witnessed surveyors across the country this summer, I have been immensely impressed by this exercise. There *are* very positive aspects, as even a cursory glance at the other chapters in this volume will confirm. For me, the strongest aspect is the way in which Land Use – UK is, refreshingly, a much more reflexive and self-conscious exercise than the earlier surveys upon which it builds. Tasks 2 and 3 of the survey, in which surveyors are asked to consider the importance of 'national issues' to their square and to note their perceptions of present and future land uses, are a welcome innovation. No doubt this reflects, in part, the emergence of a much more critical and aware discipline over the past twenty years – and, more importantly, one which learns from its failures. A great deal of research was carried out into similar exercises and they were adapted accordingly.

While I note the need for continuity between the three land-use surveys, there are problems with self-consciously building upon this tradition, and much of my argument will be based upon this aspect and divided into three foci. The first concerns technique, and whether the sampling procedure, while objective, does not reinforce dominant and conservative valuing of particular landscapes. The second is an evaluation of whether Land Use – UK really reflects the main concerns of today's discipline, questioning whether the progressivism evident in Stamp's survey is adhered to, and noting that Land Use – UK's emphasis upon environmental issues as a key concern of geographical enquiry can easily mutate into a dangerously reactionary exercise. The final summative section will deal with the concept of citizenship implicit to Land Use – UK and assess the possible uses to which it might be put in helping students to 'belong'.

Mapping valued environments

Another ITE remotely sensed survey, the Countryside Survey project, forms some of the scientific justification for Land Use – UK. The Land Use – UK surveyors in rural areas provided field data as additional ground-truth to accompany the remotely sensed data of the Countryside Survey, and the urban surveyors provided valuable data which had not been gathered previously. This represents an interesting mix of mapping techniques. Recently we have witnessed radical changes in the technology and use of maps and mapping. Satellite imaging, computer software and increasingly powerful hardware have helped redefine the nature and use of the map. Multi-dimensional perspectives and integrated applications have radically extended its functions: swathes of territory in Eastern Europe are currently being re-planned using GIS technology; landscapes and environments can now be forested, flooded, ecologically re-balanced, or developed in the virtual space of the computer, without surveyors or planners ever muddying their boots. These technical advances in mapping bring with them new perspectives on the world: removing the constraints of sheet borders, revealing less fragmented space, and indicating the linkages and movements of people, resources and cultures between places, territories and nations. But this is in tension with the tradition of land-use survey. The grounded and locally based attachments with environment which are encouraged by fieldwork exercises such as Land Use – UK can easily ignore this interconnectedness, and it is difficult to identify in the Survey Pack any suggestions of how such limitations might be overcome in the dissemination or teaching of the survey.

Unlike both previous surveys, Land Use – UK did not attempt to map every single square kilometre of land. With declining education budgets and increasing strain on teachers' time and school resources this is not surprising. However, the ITE and GA's scientific sampling of 500 rural and 500 urban key squares, while balanced, must be considered within the broader context of the survey, and particularly of Tasks 2 and 3. I have briefly noted the rural bias of Stamp's survey, and it is evident that Land Use – UK seems to have taken this particular aspect of the land-use survey tradition on board. To be true to population distribution in Britain, I suspect that a much greater number of urban squares should have been sampled. The real 'problems' at present experienced in Britain such as homelessness, poverty, crime, unemployment, and so on, are concentrated in the urban areas, and geography has a duty to address them.

The Task 2 'national issues' perhaps exacerbate this rural bias and indicate that Land Use – UK should have explored more deeply the sources and ideology of these concerns.

Of the five national issues, not one is expressly urban. New housing, for instance, concerns the 'loss of countryside', in an echo of inter-war concerns for urban sprawl and the spread of urban intrusions into rural areas. In the 1920s and 30s, urban intrusions did not simply refer to new housing but also to inappropriate elements in the visual environment, such as advertising hoardings or poorly designed street furniture. Similarly, this sentiment can be found in the fourth national issue, the existence of communication towers and pylons, and this also applies to out-of-town retail developments.

In our experience of the Land Use – UK exercise this summer, urban surveyors were left unable to consider national issues, and none of the problems in their *local* environment were deemed *nationally* important to the GA and, by association, the subject of geography itself. Given that Land Use – UK was conceived as an exercise to promote geography, this is a problem. And while I do not imply that the issues selected are not important, their selection does reflect a popular perception that the seat of national identity in Britain can be found in the idealised rural environment and that communities living in that environment somehow embody the ways of life and virtues to which, as a nation, we should aspire. In short, the message of Land Use – UK can be read cynically as being conservative, by suggesting that you do not *belong* to the nation as an active and conscientious citizen unless you can appreciate the nation's nature which is located in our countryside. Nor is it a great leap to suggest that the signs of urban decline witnessed by inner-city surveyors on Land Use – UK are in part contributed to by the symbolic importance of the rural over the urban which was easily lost beneath the 'objectivity' of the study in which they were involved.

There is a specific landscape or environment which, as an educational exercise, Land Use – UK seems to favour: the rural/urban fringe with which Stamp was most concerned. These zones are highly contested in terms of land use and are usually under development pressure. In them can be found most, if not all, of the 'national issues': new housing, out-of-town supermarkets, closed village shops, infrastructural developments such as communication towers, and the subsidised setaside land of farmers who may perhaps be waiting in the hope of selling the land to a future developer. It was no surprise to discover that students who were surveying in these areas had a keen sense of local issues, got the most out of the exercise, and, more importantly, appeared to express a greater sense of responsibility toward their environment. Here rural ways of life were perceived to be under threat and the emphasis upon these issues in the Land Use – UK instructions served to confirm their involvement in a nationally important exercise.

It is ironic, therefore, that Land Use – UK, as an exercise in learning to belong, does in fact inadvertently seem to exclude.

Environmental consciousness and progressive geography

Building upon this argument, it does seem to be the case that Land Use – UK might obscure some of the more recent concerns of geography. Implicit in the published material for the survey is the commonly held notion that the foundation of geography as a discipline is people–environment relationships. Land-use survey is founded upon a concern for the ways in which society organises the raw material of its environment and produces patterns on the ground. But frequently such surveys only produce snapshots: patterns which seem to exist for their own sake with little indication of their underlying causes – and, where those causes are explored, they rarely progress beyond the environmental. As an educational exercise this can become a problem. Dependent upon how it was taught in the field, all three tasks of Land Use – UK can be conducted without recourse to, for instance, the socio-economic and cultural processes which help explain the resultant patterns. Contemporary geography is characterised by its engagement with these types of processes as a similarly holistic study; but, by relying too heavily upon the land-use survey tradition in Britain, Land Use – UK perhaps reconstructs a much older vision of geography which might negate any progressive intent.

It must be noted that I do not believe Land Use – UK intends to be either conservative or reactionary, but by emphasising environmental issues in its teaching and analysis it could easily become so. This depends, of course, upon the educational context within which the exercise is undertaken. While, in its broadest sense, Land Use – UK is environmental education – and especially so in Tasks 2 and 3 – what constitutes environmental issues are too readily prescribed. At the root of all environmental problems lie socio-economic causes, and too often 'the protection of the environment' is motivated less by concern with the environment for its own sake than by questionable political, economic and cultural biases (consider the favouring of the rural environment above the urban noted above). 'Environment' is used in this way as an apolitical excuse for some highly political actions.

This is perhaps best demonstrated by using an example from our monitoring of the survey in the favoured environment of past surveys and of Land Use – UK: the rural/urban fringe. We chose to concentrate on these environments in south-east England where the surveyors tended to be mainly middle-class and white and keenly aware of local issues of development and environment. It was no surprise to encounter a certain amount of 'nimby-ism' among this group, but its manifestation was interesting. With a group in the field, I worked through the 'national issues' task sitting on top of a hill overlooking the square we had just surveyed. This contained a commuter village. Regarding the question of new housing over the last five years, no recent building was noted. I then asked them to tell me what the problem with new housing might be in that location. They replied that the architecture would not fit in with existing housing stock, that it would damage an ecologically sensitive area, and that 'council housing' was always poorly designed and badly built (I had not suggested to them the type or tenure of housing). Building upon this, when asked what social problems might arise by expanding the village, 'crime' was the unanimous reply. Clearly, the environment, both visual and ecological, was being used under the auspices of the Land Use – UK exercise to express social issues or, rather, to hide social prejudice. This was not an uncommon response, and I do not wish to criticise these students for repeating commonly held conceptions or for the prevalent tendency to hide political beliefs beneath apparently apolitical environmental concerns.

Similarly, different but equally reactionary responses arose when running through Task 3 ('views and visions') with a school in the de-industrialised heart of an inner-city area. There, degradation of the environment, including boarded-up shops, graffiti and vandalism, were related by the students to the racial composition of the square's inhabitants. Once again, if you dig deeper into environmental concern and begin tackling the underlying socio-economic and cultural processes, it becomes clear that 'environment' tends to obscure complicated and situated prejudices. In this situation, for instance, it is impossible to explain or teach the patterns on the ground, or address the students' attitudes towards them, without considering a range of broader economic and socio-cultural processes.

Here, I am not suggesting that I disagree with the vision of geography implicit in Land Use – UK, nor that geographers should abandon a people–environment focus. Rather, I wish to point out the pitfalls of this focus which seem clearly evident in the conduct of the survey in many different environments. Perhaps these problems arise from the ways in which Land Use – UK consciously draws upon the established survey tradition in Britain, which itself has been characterised by numerous hidden agendas.

In short, we should always deal with each environment and its attendant 'problems' from a variety of perspectives, from physical through social to cultural, emphasising the variety of processes which underlie patterns on the map.

Citizen 2000

When outlining the concept of citizenship they wish to promote, previous surveys have stressed the importance of learning to belong at the local level, and, from there, building to an appreciation of the position of the local within the national and international schema. Land Use – UK too, building upon Local Agenda 21 recommendations, states its objectives as being to promote 'greater knowledge and understanding of the local environment', and also to 'emphasise the value of survey work as a preparation for citizenship'. Citizenship is a complicated concept, and it will suffice here to note that geographers have generally worked through the notion of citizenship as engendering certain rights and responsibilities toward the environment, and, through geographical education, promoting that notion of belonging, particularly at the local level.

However, the version of local citizenship presented in Land Use – UK may not be successful, largely due to the scientific sampling process. The probability of a registered school falling within one of the 1,000 key squares was remote, and in all the key squares we monitored none were within easy reach of the school. Consequently, few of the surveyors had an awareness of specifically local issues or any sense of responsibility for the area or of belonging to it. This problem was alleviated by the local squares (not included in the final analysis). It is no coincidence, therefore, that local squares appeared to be the most successful in fulfilling the survey's aims, with students well aware of various local concerns and better able to deal with Tasks 2 and 3.

Nevertheless, the question of defining the 'local' is clearly central to issues of local citizenship, and abstract sampling and mapping procedures, if anything, tend to override any deeply felt sense of place. It is difficult to superimpose imaginary gridlines over the area you consider home, and necessarily, by framing in such a way, much of importance can be lost. In the 1930s survey, this might have been more successful, with the parish acting as the basic unit, but in Land Use – UK the sampling process perhaps excludes more of these intangible feelings than it includes. Moreover, in an era of economic and cultural globalisation it is wrong to assume that 'home' or 'locality' are fixed in time and space. By point sampling it is easy to overlook the essential interconnectedness of localities and the interconnectedness of environments from local to global scales, in the same way that the static and enframed picture presented in the 1930s and 1960s surveys hid a range of dynamic processes.

But this is not a criticism, since the whole issue of citizenship and education is fraught with danger. It is a debate which is very easy to enter into in an ill-informed manner, as recent events relating to schools in Halifax and Nottingham seem to suggest. I do not wish to end on a negative note. Despite my reservations, I recognise Land Use – UK to have been a highly ambitious and successful project. Citizenship and a sense of belonging have always been important to geography. As all the teachers we interviewed agreed, the discipline has a role to play in forming conscientious and critically aware citizens.

It is in the 'views and visions' responses that the most effective legacy of Land Use – UK will lie. It is, I think, not too presumptuous to suppose that just as echoes of Stamp's survey conclusions can be found in the 1951 Festival of Britain and in many aspects of post-war planning, so the views and visions of the 1996 surveyors will resonate with the spirit of the millennium celebrations and be of relevance well into the next century.

Chapter 15: An observer's view of Land Use – UK

Jon May

In the previous chapter Simon Rycroft discussed some of the broader issues raised by Land Use – UK. They formed the basis of a joint research project undertaken by Simon, Tony Binns and me in which we attempted to locate Land Use – UK within a longer tradition of land-use survey in this country. We sought to unpack something of the broader vision of geography which the survey hopes to promote as part of its aim of raising the profile of geography within schools and among the public.

As part of the project, we spent the summer shadowing schools in different parts of the country as they undertook the survey, and interviewed teachers and children in an attempt to uncover how the themes discussed in the previous chapter were understood and negotiated by the surveyors themselves. During the course of these interviews we were also able to learn much about the different experiences people had had of taking part in the project – not simply why they had become involved and how they had organised their survey work, but whether they had enjoyed it and their feelings about the project in general. It seemed to us that these experiences were important, not only for any future history of the discipline (autobiographical accounts of Stamp's surveyors still make fascinating reading and tell us much about the wider vision of geography circulating at the time) but for the survey designers too, inasmuch as they might form an important resource in the design of any future exercise. So although I hope this chapter will connect with the previous one, documenting how the surveyors negotiated the issues raised there, the primary focus of this chapter is on the different experiences of *doing* Land Use – UK, offering a practical assessment of the exercise and giving voice to a few of the many thousands of people who took part in it.

Getting involved

With nearly 1400 participating schools, it is clear that Land Use – UK has proved an enormously popular exercise. In itself, however, this popularity does not explain quite why so many people have embraced the project. To understand this we have to listen to the participants themselves, and talking to secondary geography teachers we find a number of reasons for their involvement.

For some teachers it offered a useful and timely way of raising the profile of geography within their schools. The fact that the project was of practical application, creating new information for use in the real world, certainly made the project easier to 'sell' to both children and other staff on the grounds that the school would be contributing to something of real significance – a theme we constantly stressed in our pre-survey briefings. Beyond this 'promotional' exercise, two other themes consistently emerged whenever teachers were asked what their main motivations were for joining Land Use – UK: fieldwork, and data collection and analysis.

Fieldwork

The continued importance of fieldwork was frequently stressed. For a long time geographers have argued that fieldwork lies at the heart of their discipline, but few attempts have been made to define precisely why practical fieldwork activities are so important. Consequently, in a climate of declining departmental budgets and increasing pressures on staff time, in the absence of a clearer definition of the value of fieldwork many schools (and universities) have seen their field activities cut back. One reason for the popularity of Land Use – UK would therefore seem to be not only that with it the GA had put the fieldwork question firmly back on the educational agenda and designed an activity with which teachers could re-introduce their students to the core benefits of it, but, crucially, that it provided a 'ready-made' exercise on which they could draw. As one of the teachers we talked to put it:

> I'd been thinking about doing some more locally based work, but things like a lack of base maps and structure that was, well, ready-made if you like, had rather held me back, because actually setting something up initially you have got to get a decent map and decide exactly what you are going to do, how you are going to do the categories and so on. But this was sort of on a plate and I thought, well, I'll give it a go.

Thinking through the benefits of fieldwork more clearly, and thus one attraction of Land Use – UK, two issues are particularly important. The first is the opportunity fieldwork affords for the development of a number of basic geographical skills – of map reading and observation, data collection and analysis. Though we might think that children would be familiar with these skills, for a number of teachers the value of Land Use – UK was quickly revealed when it became apparent how poor many of their students actually were at, for example, basic map work. One Year-8 teacher said:

> One of the things I found fascinating today was that although we had done work from Ordnance Survey maps and they seemed to have grasped it – you know, they could do good map references, find things on the map, describe routes – today they were like 'Where are we?' and they seemed to have very little concept of 'Well, we're moving down the road so this is the next place where we've got a number on the map.'

Data collection and analysis

As another teacher remarked, the sheer proliferation of secondary data that is now available to schools can mean that children are less well equipped than previous generations at sorting through that data and taking a critical attitude to the limitations of the material with which they are presented. Once again, one of the values of Land Use – UK has been that as a practical exercise it re-affirmed the importance of first-hand experience, requiring children to collect their own data and revealing to them the limitations of different collection methods and different data types. Talking to some of the young surveyors themselves, the value of this first-hand experience should not be underestimated. As one Year-8 student put it after returning from the field:

> You see, like, people counts in books and, OK, it's just a recording sheet but you need to know how they're done ... and like, say, you see a pie chart you don't realise the actual work that has gone into it, but when you try and do it yourself, you do.

The second major benefit of a fieldwork approach is the way in which it brings the often abstract concepts of the classroom to life, making them easier to grasp and allowing for an understanding of their complexity and local specificity. This is in many ways a more complex argument, and one that, in the context of Land Use – UK, needs considerable elaboration – especially given the kinds of concerns raised in the previous chapter regarding the form of the exercise through which the GA has chosen to promote geography as a discipline, not only to children but to the public at large.

These concerns relate to the GA's decision to promote geography through a mapping exercise, and to the kinds of information that Land Use – UK will produce.

Promoting geography: a progressive vision?

Geography at all levels, whether in school or university, increasingly stresses the role of process rather than simply pattern, and the interdependence of different places rather than the isolated geographies of different places or regions. There is arguably also a new 'politics' abroad (or to be more accurate, the rediscovery of an old one), not in any party-political sense, but in the sense that many practitioners feel that geography can and should be an inherently political discipline irrespective of the scale of its focus. A simple example may be its role of demonstrating the geographical dimensions of social inequality. Thus, in the schools setting, key stage 3 of the National Curriculum instructs us that children should be encouraged to 'become aware of the global context within which places are set, how they are interdependent, and how they may be affected by processes operating at different scales'.

However, in the previous chapter doubts were raised over whether, given these new concerns, Land Use – UK represents the most appropriate advertisement for a new and progressive geography. For example, it was questioned whether a mapping exercise, or at least one accessible to children of a broad range of ages and ability, could hope to capture this new-found concern with process. Similarly, it was suggested that the explicitly local focus of Land Use – UK might indicate a failure to engage with the interdependence of different places, with implications for the nature of citizenship that the exercise hopes to promote. Finally, concern was also raised over the design of the exercise itself: the categories of land use chosen for mapping and the choice of national concerns listed in Task 2. These features apparently suggest a particular political agenda rooted in *environment* – a familiar concern among geographers – rather than economic change or social inequality, and a project biased towards the rural rather than focused upon the urban.

The reason I want to raise these issues again here is not only because I happen to feel they are important, but because they are issues that were negotiated, whether implicitly or explicitly, by all those who took part in Land Use – UK, both teachers and children. Moreover, they were, I think, issues that were worked through in creative and progressive ways by the surveyors – in ways that reveal the strengths rather than the limitations of Land Use – UK itself. Taking the apparent rural bias of the survey's design, for example, it is interesting that neither the children nor the teachers we talked to identified directly with the concern. Rather, as a Year-8 pupil with a sophisticated grasp of the sampling system reminded us, the aim of the survey was to establish a representative coverage of Britain's land use by area, not by population. In this sense the survey designers were to be praised for including so many categories for urban areas. Moreover, although schools working in the urban areas often suggested that there should have been more urban categories, teachers and children in the rural squares wanted to see more categories for their areas too. What this suggests is less the identification of some simple rural bias than an agreement among almost all those we talked to that the categories in general could have been more detailed.

Here, it is interesting to note the kinds of detail that both children and teachers wished to see. Almost without exception both the surveyors and the survey leaders argued that the land-use categories should have been more finely divided so as to reveal something of the important changes that have affected the geography of the United Kingdom in recent years. For example, for one teacher in rural Sussex 'there weren't enough categories for agriculture ... arable should have been split to show some of the more modern crops that have been grown, because they show a great deal of agricultural change'. In a similar vein, both teachers and children working in urban squares consistently expressed the limitations of the residential category. They thought it should have been divided further, to show different types of housing (with the most common suggestion being a division between public and private), and they would have liked to reveal more of the function of the industrial, commercial and business categories too - for example, to distinguish between retail outlets and service or financial industries, or between different kinds of manufacturing industry. They would also have liked to be able to show scale: in the survey a corner shop employing two people was mapped under the same category as the headquarters of a major international bank.

Looking at the preliminary results of the mapping exercise it is clear that Land Use - UK has captured some of the more interesting changes to have impacted upon the geography of the United Kingdom over the past twenty years or so. One cannot help but be struck, for example, by the very low proportion of land characterised by industrial use and the higher proportion of that use now evident in rural rather than inner-city areas. Such results need to be treated with caution, of course, but would seem to provide important evidence of wider processes of economic change (see Chapter 6). But how much more interesting it would be to know the details of these changes: which industries are declining, which expanding, which industries are now located where, or which crop types now dominate Britain's arable land? Given that the children we talked to were certainly capable of using more complex categories - especially as, in practice, surveyors in any one area were deploying only a few of the categories listed - the failure to map such details is undoubtedly an opportunity missed. As one teacher noted, 'The lack of this more detailed information must limit the practical uses to which the data gathered as part of the exercise can be put.'

It is partly in response to such limitations that the previous chapter raised questions over the ability of Land Use - UK to capture, and promote, geography's increasing concern with process. The political slant of the exercise can also be called into question, and here its apparent rural bias is worth re-examining. For example, for those children we talked to who surveyed rural squares, the question of new housing was clearly identified as an issue of some concern. In contrast, for children in inner Sheffield the concern was not so much the spread of new housing as the lack of affordable housing for themselves and their families. As one of them observed 'there's all that spare countryside and so many homeless', so in what sense is the spread of new housing into the countryside a bad thing? 'It depends who it's for.' This raises questions about the list of avowedly 'national issues' recorded in Task 2, and also about the political rationale behind the nature of some of the categories. Given the number of surveyors mobilised, it does seem a pity that the exercise could not have been used to gather evidence on some other issues of current social concern - the decline of decent affordable housing, for example - evidence that might have presented the public with a more progressive image of the discipline.

At the same time, these are clearly difficult issues to resolve. For the survey designers, the choice of categories had to reflect the different ages of the participants and was to some extent driven by the lowest common denominator. In so far as the categories that were chosen had to be understood by both primary and secondary-school children, they perhaps represented the best compromise between an achievable exercise and the kind of detail that the children we talked to would have liked to have seen. Simply increasing the number of categories would not necessarily have been a fail-safe solution, as different groups in different areas would all have wished to see their particular concerns, and thus their particular understanding of geography, reflected in the survey design.

More significantly, to criticise Land Use - UK on these grounds may, anyway, be to misunderstand the true nature of the initiative. As for any fieldwork activity, the real value of Land Use - UK lies not so much in the type of data that has been collected, but in the collection of the data itself - the doing of the exercise - and in the

Townscapes old and new

Photos: Bryan Ledgard

Photo: Eurotunnel/OA Photos

The amount of land used for transport is a striking feature of the changes that have taken place since the last land-use survey in the 1960s

Photo: Keith Grimwade

subsequent classroom discussions. Here the kinds of concern with process and with politics that the children and teachers we talked to wished to see in the survey design did in fact emerge, and often in interesting ways. Moving around a square in inner London, for example, the attention of one group was drawn to recent processes of gentrification, which initiated heated discussion about the impact of such change on the children's own lives. Back in the classroom the debate moved on to the survey design – why had it not been possible to record the gentrification processes on the land-use map itself? This showed that for these children the value of Land Use – UK reflected the value of any good piece of fieldwork: its ability to generate debate about the problems and limitations of different methodologies, and to bring the abstract concepts of the classroom to life. As one student reflected, describing the contrast between rich and poor that he had seen in the square he visited, but which up to then had been encountered only in the pages of a textbook:

> *It opens your eyes to the world doesn't it – I mean before, you never really got a view of what kind of world you live in, but like now it's opened my eyes, you know, actually seeing that contrast for yourself.*

Land Use – UK and the question of citizenship

The comments of this surveyor lead us to consider how far Land Use – UK was successful in another of its aims, namely the promotion of a stronger sense of citizenship. Again, the question of citizenship is a complex one, and one that Land Use – UK sought to develop in a number of ways. First, the exercise was clearly designed to foster a sense of local citizenship through the promotion of local knowledge. Here, it is notable that in almost every school we visited both children and teachers were surprised by the ways in which doing Land Use – UK had made them look at areas they thought they knew well in new ways and had drawn their attention to a number of different local issues. Whether or not this awareness will translate into a sense of local responsibility or expand beyond a sense of local consciousness to forge connections in children's minds between the 'local' and the 'global' it is too early to tell.

One of the more interesting findings to emerge out of our research, however, was how many teachers welcomed this renewed focus on the local. Pointing to the kinds of environmental issues that dominate the media (e.g. the destruction of the rainforest or of the ozone layer) they suggested that children often have an acute sense of 'global citizenship' but a far less developed sense of responsibility for the local. In contrast to the arguments made in the previous chapter, they therefore suggested that, rather than being restrictive, this focus on local responsibility offered an important counterpoint to the ways in which questions of citizenship have tended to develop in recent years, and they broadly welcomed the scale of focus at which Land Use – UK operated.

However, the concept of citizenship hinges around questions of rights as well as responsibilities, and, in the context of Land Use – UK, this shift in emphasis entails a further shift in the scale at which we address questions of citizenship and assess the success of the project. One of the major 'selling points' of Land Use – UK was that it would apparently offer the chance for children to give voice to their concerns, most obviously through Task 3, with the implicit understanding that their opinions would be listened to by people working at national level with the power to shape the ways in which Britain's land use develops. Looking at the feelings of the surveyors themselves, however, it is clear that children's belief in their right to be listened to differs in important ways according not only to class but also according to where they live – and the two often work together, of course. Compare, for example, the responses in the panel to the question of what the survey was for and for whom it was designed: the

JM: Why do you think they want a map like this?
Tonbridge pupil: To show the difference between places in England and to make it more tidy.
JM: Why do you think it will help make it more tidy?
Tonbridge pupil: Because they can see what the problems are.
JM: Do you think they will listen to you?
Tonbridge pupil: They should do. It's what they set it up for isn't it?

JM: Why do you think they want all this information?
Sheffield pupil: So the government can see where the countryside is and build more (expensive) houses on it.

JM: Why do you think they want all this information?
London pupil: They're only going to choose someone's 'views and visions' that are like the same as theirs, so it doesn't really matter what you put.

first set from a Year-8 pupil in Tonbridge, Kent, and the others from inner-city Year-9 students, one in inner Sheffield and the other in inner London.

What these responses make plain is that, for those who not only feel marginalised but who are in very real ways both socially and politically marginalised, there is a long way to go before we are likely to see the development of a stronger sense of citizenship. For these children the ability of an exercise like Land Use – UK to help in this development is perhaps limited, and not least as the exercise was perceived as connecting more strongly with the interests and needs of the child living in Tonbridge than of the two from Sheffield and London. At a conceptual level this reconnects us to the question of whether or not Land Use – UK represents the best advertisement for geography we can make, either to the public at large or to children themselves. At a more immediate level it also provides a link to consider a few of the practical problems the exercise encountered.

Land Use – UK: a practical assessment

Given the scale of Land Use – UK, and the time frame within which the project was carried out, at a national level the exercise undoubtedly represents a logistical triumph. On the ground, however, the experience was often rather different. If only to help with the organisation of any future initiatives, it is worth looking in detail at a few of the problems that different schools encountered. First, though in general the teachers we talked to reported that their schools had in the main been very supportive of the exercise, and that arranging the survey had not been difficult, logistical problems did still emerge. Most obviously, the size of the exercise meant that a number of departments were dependent upon using non-geographers as survey leaders, which led to difficulties in the field. Some teachers had problems arranging cover for the period in which both they and the children were out of school. Others suggested that the GA had underestimated the time involved in preparing the survey work, both for themselves and for the children, and even the costs involved in conducting the survey. Sometimes the amount of photocopying placed a strain on already tight departmental budgets.

Constraints of time meant that few teachers were able to set aside class time to work through the broader issues with which the survey was connecting in any detail. This often left children and other staff with only a vague idea of why they were doing it – correcting the Ordnance Survey base map being a popular misconception. Even fewer teachers were able to attend the organised training sessions, and – despite the fact that all praised the survey instructions, which were thought to be very clear – in the field this led to problems of accuracy. This was a particular problem when non-geographers were faced with an ambiguous categorisation such as deciding between derelict land and land in transition.

Third, problems of accuracy were worsened by the allocation procedure. Of the schools we visited only two had been allocated key squares immediately adjacent to the school, and many had a considerable distance to travel. While this created logistical difficulties, it also meant that in practice few were able to draw upon any local knowledge. This in turn meant that in both the urban and rural squares it often became difficult to identify the national issues, particularly what was or was not setaside land, and which houses had been built within the last five years. Overall, the urban results should perhaps be treated with a certain caution. Often the density of settlement and the scale of the base maps meant that recording quickly changing land uses was difficult, while the instruction to note only ground-floor use meant that the recorded category often did not tally with the main use of a particular area: where a twelve-storey residential block stood atop a set of shops, for example.

Finally, in our observations we found that the practice of survey leaders differed markedly across the country. Most worrying, in terms of the accuracy of the information collected, was that only two of the eight or so leaders we worked with had any plans to revisit their survey square to check their results, pointing again to the difficulties raised by allocation. In a another vein, different teachers interacted in very different ways with their survey teams. The most successful were those who worked with their pupils, leading groups around the square and using the exercise as an opportunity to draw the attention of their students to different issues in the local area, but leaving the children themselves to carry out the survey exercise. Others – especially non-geographers – tended to do the surveying themselves, leaving the children to simply drag behind, uninterested in the exercise or in the area they were moving through. How far such practices were repeated across the country is difficult to assess, but I have raised them here because they seem to me to lie at the heart of the benefits of Land Use – UK, namely the initiative's wider educational potential.

Conclusions

When assessing the overall success of Land Use – UK, one of the most important things is whether or not those involved in the project enjoyed it (in general a resounding Yes!); whether or not it can be considered to have been a useful educational exercise, and whether or not it represents the kind of image of geography we would like to see presented to both future geographers and the public more widely.

I have already suggested that there are a number of problems with the image of geography that Land Use – UK is promoting. Most obvious are its apparent lack of concern with questions of process, the general nature of the information it has generated, and its failure to move beyond a rather traditional focus upon the environment towards an examination of other issues of public concern. These are issues to which geographers can offer a unique insight: for example, the nature and extent of recent agricultural, economic and social change. The omissions may mean that both the public and the children will continue to see geography as a rather old-fashioned discipline that has little to say about a number of the more pressing issues of the day.

However, I have also tried to suggest that in many ways Land Use – UK did create space for an examination of these more progressive issues in terms of the questions and debates that were raised by the children we talked to while surveying. Getting children out of the classroom and into their local areas brought them face-to-face with processes of local and global change, and forced them to think about the problems and possibilities connected to the different methods of measuring and analysing that change. More significantly, in doing the exercise children up and down the country have begun to look at their local areas in new ways, have gained an appreciation of the different issues facing these areas, and, crucially, have started to think about what their role as geographers and citizens might be in confronting them.

This, it seems to me, is what geography should be all about, and they are values which are most easily conferred through fieldwork. Therefore the most lasting benefit of Land Use – UK may be that it has placed the issue of fieldwork firmly back at the heart of the educational agenda, and at a practical level has furnished teachers with an invaluable fieldwork resource on which to draw in future years. Here it is significant that almost every one of the teachers we talked to planned to adapt the exercise for future use, turning a resource designed to be applicable to a range of pupils in a number of settings into something more directly applicable to their own local curriculum needs. In a world of declining budgets and growing pressure on staff time the GA should congratulate itself on offering something of real value to its members. The question for the future, of course, is whether anyone has the energy to conduct such an exercise again. Let us all hope they have!

Photo: Paula Richardson

Chapter 16: In retrospect

Rex Walford

Even though some field-results are still trickling in and the final accounts have yet to be determined, the bulk of the survey has been done and this is a good opportunity to look back on Land Use – UK.

The results

Part 2 (Chapters 5–8) presents the results of the initial analysis of the data gathered during the summer of 1996. Data from more than 1500 key and local squares all over the UK has so far been returned, and most of it is now stored in a computer database. Besides the actual survey maps returned in paper form, the database includes the patterned returns of the sampling of 100 points of data on each square. This considerable resource awaits further research and it is to be hoped that finance can be found for scholars to investigate it further.

The commentary provided in Part 2 has already drawn attention to some of the more striking findings and made some comparisons with past surveys. Part of the Land Use – UK survey data will take its place in the record of knowledge about the UK environment, but the Task 3 returns ('views and visions') are a genuinely innovative contribution and have already attracted considerable interest from beyond the project. They provide a wide-ranging insight into the way in which a large number of young people view the contemporary environment, and their richness has yet to be fully explored.

The form and structure of Land Use – UK

One reservation expressed about the form of the survey was that by working with individual kilometre-grid squares some of the more complex synoptic patterns and issues in the environment might be overlooked or underplayed. 'Isn't one of the strengths of geography its ability to see the wider perspective? Might you not be compromising that by going for survey of small-scale parcels of environment?' said one university academic, commenting on the form of the survey at a training meeting. There is certainly some force in that criticism, but it has to be balanced against the advantages conferred by the sample-square method. The latter made a comprehensive survey within one summer practicable, and was the focus for the discussions held by teachers and their classes. It did not preclude consideration of wider issues.

In some parts of the country there were concerted projects to map a block of squares in order to see the wider framework (see Chapters 12 and 13). A notable initiative in Knowsley saw the whole of the district surveyed by local schools and the results put to good use by the local authority strategic planning team. GA branches and other local authorities also have plans to extend the Land Use – UK method to larger areas.

The size and structure of Land Use – UK also needs to be put in perspective alongside other recent surveys. The Countryside Survey of 1990, organised by ITE, recorded 508 one-kilometre squares – 16 or more per Land Class – and gave details about land cover, land use and land management. The 1996 Land Use – UK survey, using a similar Land Class stratification, has examined so far 418 additional rural key squares and a further 553 rural local squares, making a total of 1479 rural squares generated by the two surveys. In addition Land Use – UK has covered 410 key squares of an entirely new urban class and added another 147 urban local squares. Although between them the two surveys have recorded only 1% of Britain's landscape, the sample is securely based on an environmental stratification which allows the generation of detailed regional and national maps of the land with confidence.

The survey demonstrated the advantages of computer analyses of map data – advantages that were not routinely available previously, even at the time of Alice Coleman's 1960s survey. Computer analysis helped the project team to produce maps and data quickly and efficiently, and the figures and tables in this book represent a small sample of the results that can be generated from the database compiled.

The Countryside Information System (a Microsoft Windows program) was designed especially for scaling up the results of the ITE sample surveys of 1978, 1984 and 1990, and can be similarly applied to Land Use – UK. The maps and graphs in this book have been generated using the CIS program.

Bias?

There was some criticism of Task 2 of the survey – that the recording of so-called 'national issues' was biased towards the rural. Simon Rycroft expands upon this in detail in Chapter 14. This passage gives the flavour of the argument:

> In our experience of the Land Use – UK exercise this summer, urban surveyors were left unable to consider national issues, and none of the problems in their local environment were deemed nationally important to the GA and, by association, the subject of geography itself. Given that Land Use – UK was conceived as an exercise to promote geography, this is a problem. And while I do not imply that the issues selected are not important, their selection does reflect a popular perception that the seat of national identity in Britain can be found in the idealised rural environment and that communities living in that environment somehow embody the ways of life and virtues to which, as a nation, we should aspire.

Rycroft raises a significant issue which runs well beyond the confines of this particular survey. The issues chosen for Task 2 were those most frequently suggested by teachers themselves in preliminary discussions, and which no doubt reflected their concerns and those of their pupils. To that extent they are not surprising, because they have their origin inside the rural-oriented frame which Rycroft characterises as a 'popular perception'. What is at tension here is the validity of that perception and what Rycroft, by inference, believes that geography's present foci of study should represent – foci more representative of the urban world.

Perhaps Land Use – UK can take refuge in the stance that to promote geography it does not necessarily have to be positioned to reflect all geographical interests, and that some of the 'urban issues' which might otherwise have been addressed (e.g. the extent of the provision of low-cost affordable housing, gentrification etc.) would be much less practicable to identify and survey accurately, given the disparate age and experience of survey teams involved.

It might also be argued that concern about the fate of the 'countryside' is as fundamental a national issue as the state of the urban fabric. In February 1996 it caused the rarest of political events – a joint letter to *The Times*, signed by the leaders of all three major British political parties, John Major, Tony Blair and Paddy Ashdown.

During the next few months, we shall differ on so many problems of public importance that we gladly take the opportunity of showing that on one subject we speak with a united voice – namely in advocating the protection of our countryside in its rich personality and character. We do this in the full confidence that necessary development can and should be directed with thoughtful and scrupulous attention to the charm of our countryside. Much of its beauty is the direct result of man's activities in the past: and in these days when the objectives of planning and land management and the appreciation of landscape are more widely shared than ever before, we ought to be able to make necessary changes in ways that avoid injuring our precious heritage.

An immediate riposte came the following day from a Cambridge academic who pointed out that the last time an all-party letter of support for the countryside was sent to *The Times* (by Baldwin, MacDonald and Lloyd George in 1929) it was followed by a decade which saw two million houses built with little regard to their surroundings or their impact on the environment.

The sharp eye of Simon Jenkins, an experienced environmental commentator, picked up some of the issues a few days later:

Last October's Rural White Paper, despite its enthusiasm for reviving villages, was meant to let developers off the leash, to convert fields into houses and businesses ... the politics of the countryside will never be anaesthetised by cross-party letters to The Times *... sensible planning would encourage housing and commerce on vacant and derelict land. Of this there is plenty in all parts of Britain, in addition to the 800,000 houses currently lying empty in England alone. There is no 'balance' to be struck in this matter. There is the countryside, glorious, shrinking, to be enjoyed by all of us only while it lasts. Once gone it is gone for ever, and no market forces can drag it back.*

The organisation and execution of Land Use – UK

Feelings of relief and elation that the organisation of Land Use – UK seemed to work well and that no major hitches occurred should not prevent scrutiny of the arrangements and procedures with the benefits of hindsight. There is no doubt that the central organisation of the project relied enormously on four major contributions:

- the time and labour charitably given by ITE scientists and some academic geographers beyond their own regular duties
- the temporary extra burden cheerfully shouldered by GA Headquarters staff
- the enterprise and adaptability of the various temporary helpers employed for various periods at Sheffield and at Monks Wood
- the consistent support and effort of the volunteer National Steering Committee and a small number of other GA members who played key roles in helping to allocate, organise and analyse.

These contributions had to be much greater than was originally expected because Land Use – UK did not have a large commercial sponsor.

Financial constraints

It was originally estimated that Land Use – UK would need a major sponsor to underwrite the project (finance for a budget of over £70,000 was sought). Despite a thorough and professional campaign we were unable to attract one. Fortunately, late in the day, we gained the support of certain charitable trusts which helped to ameliorate the position.

The chief casualty in the restriction on finance was the aborted appointment of two full-time staff members – a Project Officer and a Project Secretary. These posts had been deemed essential by most of our friends and advisers at the start of planning, and would have greatly reduced the burdens elsewhere. However, a variety of stop-gap measures were successful in keeping the administration of the project running and producing material to meet its critical publication deadlines. Much thinking on the project had to be done by the National Steering Committee through phone-ins and face-to-face meetings (ten in all), and at the end of the day the absence of a full-time officer seemed to have been successfully 'covered' in relation to essential tasks.

The Survey Handbook received general approval for its clarity and comprehensiveness, and the charging of a modest registration fee to participants (to defray some of the costs) did not seem to deter even the smallest of schools. Following the publication of the launch articles in January 1996, registrations met and eventually exceeded expectations, reaching a total of over 1400.

A small number of registering schools failed either to confirm their participation or to send back their results, despite dogged chasing from GA Headquarters. Some cited a delay in the arrival of their local map from the Ordnance Survey as an excuse, though enterprising schools in this position quickly found ways of acquiring a map of their allocated square from other sources. One suspected that those quoting delay as their reason for non-activity might have cooled in their ardour for the survey for other reasons. Most disappointing to the central organisation team were a small number of schools who had been eager to take on a number of key squares at the start, who had been given the allocation they wanted, but who then, late in the summer term, reported that they could not survey after all. The frustration was caused by the fact that such key squares could easily have been allocated elsewhere if only they had been returned earlier.

In the latter part of the project, Russell Chapman did sterling work in recruiting members of the Geographical Task Force and persuading them to retrieve some of these situations, though he often made at least half-a-dozen attempts to allocate the more distant of the remaining squares. The work of these volunteers in the remotest locations of the kingdom retrieved some potential difficulties for the project in terms of its comprehensiveness of coverage. The final figure of some 10% of designated key squares unsurveyed has not invalidated the survey, and there is hope that these areas may eventually be completed in 1997.

At the local level

Part 3, *Experiences*, and Chapter 9 in particular, is eloquent testimony to the enthusiasm engendered by the survey at local level and to the support which it received from teachers and school pupils alike.

Many teachers wrote accompanying letters to their return of results, and in the overwhelming majority of cases reported, teachers found time to prepare their students adequately as well as to debrief them on their return. The greater flexibility of summer-term timetables enabled fieldwork to be undertaken in school time in some cases, though there are plenty of examples of work done in the evenings and at the weekends by enthusiasts anxious to ensure the proper completion of the task.

Jon May, in Chapter 15, draws attention to some logistical and procedural problems which he found when observing at the local level, such as the use of non-specialist geographers as leaders (in primary schools this might even be the teacher in charge of the survey), time difficulties and questions of accuracy of survey.

In relation to the last point, the 1996 survey did at least go beyond its predecessors in providing not only a Survey Handbook but also training meetings and a helpline for support and advice during the main weeks of the survey. But, as with all surveys, those at the chalk-face inevitably uncovered circumstances which would have required the wisdom of Solomon to resolve. For example, a group of Yorkshire teachers raised the knotty point of whether bed-and-breakfast establishments in seaside resort towns such as Scarborough and Bridlington should be classified as 'residential' or 'commercial'. Even citing the criterion of 'dominant use' as the determining factor could not quench or resolve the discussion, given the nuances of economics and finance involved.

Similarly, one recognises the validity of the point that the categorisations may not, as finally formed, have fully represented the variety of urban land uses. But decisions here had to be taken in relation to what was believed to be practicable for the majority of surveyors. The question of recording 'shops' as a separate category of commercial use was given considerable discussion by the Survey Design team before the decision was made. An even larger issue was recognised – that of the recording of variety of usage in the vertical dimension of buildings – but despite much pondering no practical or simple solution was found that could satisfactorily incorporate it into the survey plan.

In Chapter 15 May also makes the point that the allocation of pre-designated key squares to schools often required them to travel some distance from their own location and that this did not help appreciation of the issues of the local environment. It is certainly true that key squares did not usually accord directly with a school's location, but the great majority were within a 10-kilometre radius of it. We also have evidence that many schools surveyed their own immediate locality for comparison with their designated key square.

Also, it should not be forgotten that the number of local squares surveyed (we have returns on the national database for 700, but there were almost certainly more) is almost equal to the number of surveyed key squares. Of necessity, the preliminary results of the survey have concentrated on the key squares, and most of the responses from the local squares await further investigation. They represent the opinions (the 'views and visions') expressed by the surveyors working in their own immediate neighbourhoods, and it will be interesting to see if these differ markedly from those analysed so far (see Chapter 8) from the sample-selected key squares.

The intentions and implications of Land Use – UK

The valuable reflections of Rycroft and May (Chapters 14 and 15) also raise some wider issues about the intentions and implications of the project.

One point made reflects a recurring dialectic in contemporary education as a whole, as well as in contemporary geography: what is the proper balance between pattern and process? At one point May asks:

> ... whether a mapping exercise, or at least one accessible to children of a broad range of ages and ability, could hope to capture this new-found concern with process.

The honest answer may well be 'no', or, at least, ' not in its primary focus', but that is neither to belittle the importance of an understanding of the dynamics of the modern world nor to imply that the exercise was incapable of fostering such insights. The decision to follow the traditional paths of the Stamp and Coleman surveys in mapping the landscape was taken partly because the language of the map itself is an essential part of the basic heritage of geography.

In completing the tasks of the project, many teachers found that the experience of taking children out into the field with maps to complete a specific task both reinforced the value and the importance of this distinctive medium of communication and provoked discussion about it. Even at the simple level of correct orientation and identification of features, formative lessons were learned by many. Schoolteachers would argue (or should argue) that mapping is a distinctive part of what geography offers to education and that teaching it is an important part of the subject's justification for remaining in the National Curriculum.

Thus, the mapping emphasis of Task 1 in Land Use – UK was construed as necessary to put in place a building-block in the house of geographical education for many of the young surveyors. The task was seen as helping the development of a fundamental skill, needed as a preliminary to the interrogation of patterns on the map or to any discernment of processes which form the pattern.

A point has also been raised concerning the role of the project in relation to citizenship. One of the approved objectives of Land Use – UK (see Chapter 1) was 'to emphasise the value of the survey for citizenship', but the generality of the language rather masks the immense ambiguities and imponderables involved in such a brief sentence.

As Rycroft points out, Stamp was clear in his mind about the fact that land-use survey could contribute to citizenship, defined in modernist terms with regard both to a national perspective and to a policy which would lead to an agreed harmonisation of people's activities and the natural environment.

Where we stand in relation to citizenship sixty years on, at the edge of a new millennium, is an altogether more problematic matter. On one hand there is the issue of what degree of belonging to locality is sensed by globe-trotters, long-distance commuters, second-home owners or the young homeless; on the other, the question of 'national identity' is confused by devolutional issues, European linkages and global influences.

The team which devised Land Use – UK were well aware of the issues, but were concerned primarily to provide room for responses from the surveyors which might shed light on perceptions currently held. Hence the inclusion of the 'views and visions' section within the survey, a distinctive addition compared with the two previous surveys in which school pupils had been involved.

More reflective and thorough analysis of that part of the survey waits to be done, as does analysis of the questionnaire circulated to participating teachers in January 1997 which asked them, among other things, how far they thought Land Use – UK had met its enigmatically expressed 'citizenship' objective.

In the interviews at the end of this book, both E. C. Willatts and Alice Coleman profess no pre-determined ulterior motives for their surveys, other than the desire to 'see what was there'. The view of later commentators is that some subtext to this emerges in the way in which the careers of the distinguished leading participants were later channelled (Stamp and Willatts towards a range of planning issues at different scales, Coleman towards large-scale urban improvement) and in the way in which even the minutiae of particular decisions appear when scrutinised from a later perspective (for example, the stark colour chosen to represent urban development on maps). This commentary is the geographical equivalent of some forms of structuralist literary criticism.

Accepting the legitimacy of that stance, it is difficult to gainsay Rycroft and May when they point out that geography is 'an inescapably political discipline' and that there are bound to be political implications in the way in which Land Use – UK was constructed and operated. But the intentions, at least as they were consciously understood, were worked through by the National Steering Committee and by GA Council, and stand as a measure by which the success or failure of the enterprise may be judged. There was certainly no party-political agenda at the forefront of the discussions and the planning. The participation of a government minister in a survey day was balanced by the leadership of several survey groups in the field by teachers who were opposition-party prospective parliamentary candidates.

The educational spin-offs from Land Use – UK

It is too early to judge what lasting spin-offs may occur from the mobilisation of so many school survey parties in the summer of 1996, but it has already been revealing to notice some of the benefits which have become apparent.

Teachers report a stimulated or renewed interest in fieldwork which they hope to continue and build upon. In the midst of increasing internal pressures, this new determination may be timely and significant given the financial and timetable constraints which may be put upon geographical work in the next few years.

There is also reported fresh interest in 'locality studies', often founded on the fact that Land Use – UK groups discovered phenomena in the neighbourhoods of their schools about which they had hitherto been unaware. This is perhaps understandable in relation to the exploration of insignificant alleyways or the revelation of small ponds, but more surprising when it relates to sports grounds, drop-forging factories and abattoirs.

For many primary teachers who had not trained as geography specialists but who were committed to the promotion of geography in school as newly appointed co-ordinators to deal with National Curriculum requirements, the survey provided a timely exemplification of the subject. 'Twinning' with another school to share results was especially popular in this sector. It has been heartening to find the number of teachers who have received the Survey Handbook as an in-service training resource and who see its role as helping them develop their own skills and understanding as well as those of their children. A number of letters to the survey organisers report that teachers intend to follow up their 1996 survey work with repeat activities in following years – and that Land Use – UK has been the spur to the start of the development of a local-studies resource.

In secondary schools, where survey leaders were more likely to be specialist-trained, there has also been widespread appreciation of the reminder of land use as a significant theme in geographical studies and of the provision of a worked-through classification system which can be applied in a variety of other contexts in the future. The Survey Handbook is to be revised and made available as a general publication by the GA.

For pupils, too, the enjoyment and vividness of the experience has been widely reported. Only time will tell if those who took part in the 1996 survey will recall with clarity and pleasure their experiences thirty years on – as did senior teachers and helpers who had taken part in the 1960s survey.

Will anybody be listening ...

May records in Chapter 15 a meeting with one group of pupils from an inner-city school who were cynical about whether their 'views and visions' would be listened to by anyone.

One can only report that, with the aid of a professional PR firm, copies of the preliminary results have already been distributed widely to television, radio, the press, government departments, opposition MPs, pressure groups, old uncle David Bellamy and all.

As well as the expected courteous acknowledgement, a letter sent to the Minister for the Environment produced this detailed reply from a senior official in the Planning and Land Use Statistics Branch of his Department:

> *DoE is very interested to see the results of the Land Use – UK Survey. The GA and its supporters for this project are very much to be congratulated on their remarkable achievement of co-ordinating such a large exercise of data collection by schoolchildren ... we are particularly interested to see the information on urban squares as there is no other source for this type of data ... we very much look forward to seeing the book that will be published next year.*

Photo: Rex Walford

Dr Christie Willatts, Secretary
of the First Land Utilisation
Survey, with David Cooper,
leader of the Land Use - UK
Results Team, in 1996

Chapter 17: The first land-use survey, in the 1930s

Rex Walford in conversation with Dr E.C.Willatts OBE, the Organising Secretary of the First Land Utilisation Survey

Twice before in this century schools have been involved in major surveys of the nation's land use. In 1929 L. Dudley Stamp, then 31 years old and Reader in Economic Geography at the London School of Economics, had been impressed by the completed maps of a county-wide survey of land use carried out by Northamptonshire schools. He was involved with a Geographical Association committee on regional surveys at the time, and initiated some preliminary discussions within this committee before going on to organise and direct an independent national land-use survey of Britain.

Dr Edward Christie Willatts joined the Survey and served as its Organising Secretary from 1931 to 1942 before going on to be a Senior Research Officer in the Planning Department of the Ministry of Works, and, from 1948, Principal Planner in the Department of the Environment until his retirement in 1973. Rex Walford visited him at his home in Horton, near Slough, in June 1996.

RW: How did you first become involved with the Survey?

ECW: I bumped into Dudley Stamp in the corridors of LSE one day in October 1931. I had graduated from LSE in 1930, and got a Teachers' Diploma in 1931. It was very difficult to pick up jobs in those days.

Dudley said, 'What are you doing, Willatts?'

I said that I had just been offered a job at Hulme Grammar School, Manchester.

'Do you want to go there?'

'I'll go where the work is.'

'Well now, what about the Land Utilisation Survey? You are already doing some of the fieldwork on the Surrey sheets. The Secretary's job is vacant. Would you like it? It's worth £200 a year but it's only guaranteed until next summer.'

So I thought – get one job, get another! I stayed ten years.

RW: What did being Secretary involve?

ECW: I made sure that the work got done – either through County Education Officers or through other volunteers. I went down to a number of counties to persuade the County Education Committee that this was a thing they should undertake in their own interest as well as ours. In the counties where the CEO was sold on the idea, they organised it all and one didn't have direct contact. But there were a number of counties that just didn't play, so we set about finding volunteers in other ways. In some places we did it school by school – a tedious business because it took many schools to cover a county. But the idea of using school pupils was there from the beginning because of the Northamptonshire example.

We had to get other gaps done by volunteers. Some universities undertook a block of work, and we persuaded countless students of the Joint School of Geography at Kings-LSE to do their bit. There came a stage when we said we would offer suitable students a subsidy of £1 a week for youth-hostel expenses or camping if they would do some work. The Lands End sheet was very largely covered by a very good group of graduate students who went down there with bicycles and camped. Somewhere in the file there is a clipping from a chap who did a great deal in Scotland: confronted with a query on the other side of a very long lake, instead of cycling round he stripped off and swam across. That's enthusiasm for you!

RW: There is an estimate somewhere that over 10,000 schools and 250,000 children were involved. When Stamp spoke about the survey at the RGS in 1931 someone asked him if it was really wise to involve schoolchildren in serious survey work, and he replied that it was his view that, from early returns, accuracy of survey work varied inversely with age! Was that just a neat answer or was it really true?

ECW: There was good evidence that the kids could do very good work: after all, they tended to be the people who knew those fields better than anybody. One saw this evidence when the crops were written in detail (not just as arable or grass) with details about hedges and fences and supplementary information – which we encouraged. You could tell instinctively after some experience whether a sheet was well surveyed or not.

RW: Was there a minimum area which people were asked to survey?

ECW: One thing that worried me when I took over was some of the literature suggesting that a parish was a useful unit. If you got a map back and there was only the information about a parish on it, you would have to multiply that by the number of parishes on 22,000 sheets and so we would have had problems!

So we stressed that the 'quarter sheet' map on the six-inch scale (total area 6 square miles) was the minimum unit and that it had to be surveyed right to the edges. That was important because when you came to edit the stuff you would bring the edges of two sheets together. That was the area that was least likely to be correctly observed: if the edges agreed, your estimation of the quality of the work went up.

Some terrain was much more difficult than others. The peneplain of Cornwall was the devil of a thing: you would be standing on gateposts to see what the land use was in the fields half of the time – and bits of Scotland also presented problems.

RW: How did you train the surveyors?

ECW: We produced a leaflet. In it we put a section of a completed map to show how it should be done. One of the disastrous things in the first stuff that went out before my time was the decision to use the letter M for the recording of meadow or grassland and W for unproductive (waste) land. If you are in the field, you are likely to turn the map round a good deal and write on it from different angles, so what were Ms and what were Ws sometimes became very hard to tell ...

We did some checking, of course. Dudley bought a car with a sunshine roof through which, standing up on the passenger seat, he viewed the countryside while his wife drove him around. He would also say to me, 'Look, I'm going to take such and such a train – give me some of the sheets I'm passing through.' Looking out of the train window you get a view that none of your volunteers had, and you could check as you went along. That was a very good way of checking. He didn't go out to do it for that reason alone, but if he was going somewhere he would make good use of his time, as he always did.

A volunteer in the first land-use survey in 1933, photographed by Dr Willatts. 'When George had done what he could from his vantage point, I, as a farmer's son, rebuked him for standing on the middle of the gate instead of at the hinge end, where his weight would do it less harm ...'

RW: When he was at LSE in the 1930s, did he get time off to manage the Survey or was he doing a full-time academic job?

ECW: He certainly was! But remember, the Survey office was at LSE where he worked.

RW: How many other employees of the Survey were there besides you?

ECW: Well, the numbers grew. When I first went there was just a typist and one girl, a cartographer. Then we got in another cartographer very quickly because there was a deluge of stuff coming in, and we had to scrutinise every sheet and mark it off on an index map if it was complete and record in manuscript form the list of surveyors. We got another girl in, then another and another; one of them was Eunice Bicknell who later became Chief Technician at LSE – a very able cartographer.

One of the main things we had to do was to transfer the information from the six-inch sheets to the one-inch scale. The Director-General of the Ordnance Survey was so keen about this that he had a set of the six-inch sheets of our first completed area, Surrey, photographed down to one-inch scale with the idea of providing the framework for the field boundaries. But it didn't work. We quickly abandoned that line and said we would do it by eye.

I pointed out to the girls that the thing to do if you got a straight boundary was to project that line to another point and make sure you get the *angle* right. It was all reduced by hand and eye to the one-inch scale and I think it was pretty soundly done. We played about with a pantograph once – dreadful instrument! Anyway, it was very much better to enlist people who could read a map well.

RW: And you were Organising Secretary for ten years?

ECW: I worked full-time from 1931 till 1939, when I was asked to take on a part-time lectureship at Birkbeck College. That involved me in working one day a week less. Then in 1941 I was asked to join the incipient Ministry of Town and Country Planning and I gave up the Birkbeck post and did the LUS part-time.

In 1942 my home here in Horton became the Survey's headquarters because we were blitzed out of London and we had to be somewhere for the first year. I was half-time with the Ministry and half-time running the LUS from here, dodging bombs about the place, being in the Home Guard and fire-watching at Birkbeck, as well as bringing up a family. Life was pretty full. All the correspondence was handled here, and a spare bedroom was turned into a drawing-office.

We had outposts elsewhere, with people reducing the field maps to the one-inch scale in places like Norwich and Nottingham. I remember writing a detailed description for them of how to overcome various problems. We did eventually get the whole lot done.

RW: When was the Survey eventually wound up then?

ECW: The last county report was published in 1946 and the last one-inch sheets published in 1949. I remember that we organised a celebration dinner for Dudley in 1947. H. J. Fleure, then Chairman of the Royal Society's National Committee for Geography, made a speech and Dudley replied.

RW: The field maps are still available in the LSE library, I believe?

ECW: In so far as they were kept together and survived the time in the 1960s when Danny the Red and other unpleasant characters were causing trouble at LSE. They opened the map chest drawers and set light to them as far as they could, and a number got charred at the edges.

RW: Stamp said in one of his books 'The Land Utilisation Survey of Britain for the 1930s was often compared with the Domesday survey, but it had no ulterior motive such as Domesday had in the matter of taxation. Its object was simply to record the factual position.' Wouldn't it be true that there was a subtext, however, in the sense that Stamp was initially concerned about the misuse of land?

ECW: No. I think that emerged from discovering the facts. I don't think he had that in mind at all when he started. It just became evident, not least when we discovered that some parts of the country were farmed in such a bad way that the land was abandoned.

RW: In the survey all the urban and industrial land was lumped into just two categories. Did you or Dudley later wish that you had categorised the urban landscape in greater detail?

ECW: You can always have those wishes, but you would never have got it done with the people we could use. It would have been more difficult to do – more likely to involve much more subjective judgement. And of course there is much more urban land now than there was then, and people are more interested in it.

RW: One of the lasting memorials to the First LUS are the invaluable County Memoirs which Stamp edited. Were those always part of the plan?

ECW: Not initially. But once we had got a county covered by survey sheets, Stamp said 'We must get something written about this.' I drew up a simple scheme for county authors, including a list of the things which they ought to cover and options which they might consider, such as looking back at the past and making comparisons and so on. We thought in terms of about 10,000 words, though the first report we got ran to 60,000 since the chap was doing it for an MA thesis!

RW: Was there much government interest before the Second World War?

ECW: I don't think there was any. But when the war came, the government set up War Agricultural Committees charged with the responsibility to ensure that we got maximum food production out of the land. These committees were empowered to tell farmers to plough up the land or else! Dudley offered the central government the use of the field sheets, and Audrey Clark and I wrapped up masses of them and despatched them. This, in effect, forged a link with the Ministry of Agriculture.

RW: War changed attitudes, presumably. A great emphasis on the need for planning came through post-war didn't it?

ECW: Absolutely. Churchill wasn't frightfully interested. But the cities were being blitzed, so he said 'We'll have to do something about planning!'

RW: Can I take up another issue? Soon after you became Organising Secretary you wrote (in *Geography*, 1932) 'The value of such work needs no reiteration in geography. The valuable training in map-reading, in accurate observation and the recording of observations, the interest evoked in the local environment leading to a realisation of civic consciousness, are well known.' And elsewhere Stamp talked about it being a great training for citizenship and the youngsters learning to appreciate their own local surroundings. Was that a large part of the survey's intention, or just a by-product?

ECW: You can never tell what benefits may flow from accumulating facts and putting them in order. The children could see where their town was sprawling, where you were getting ribbon development along a road, where it would be much better if you had a well-organised housing estate. They could begin to see what big things were happening under their very noses. When you get something down on the map, you can see the pattern and think about it.

RW: You've seen the survey instructions for the 1996 Land Use – UK project. Do you have any comments about what we are doing?

ECW: I think the art of perfecting sampling has improved enormously over the years, so it is now possible, with well-organised surveys, to get a great deal of information from sample surveys instead of comprehensive ones. Comprehensive ones can easily run into the sands by being over-ambitious and I don't need to quote any examples ...

I think you'll be able to produce valuable information by putting your percentages through computers. And you've got this 'views and visions' sheet – you're asking your volunteers to *think*, as well as *do* – I think this is splendid: you're provoking thought.

One of the question marks in my mind is how long it will take to explore the information that you gather. It always takes much longer than you think.

But basically it's the same business – going out and getting your boots muddy.

RW: Looking back, do you think your survey had a significance in British geography and British life?

ECW: In 1983 Sir Clifford Darby, the doyen of British geographers, writing of our survey, said that 'without doubt it was the greatest achievement of British geography to date'.

RW: It was a mammoth task, but the whole survey was completed and a memoir published for every county in Britain. In terms of basic organisation, it looks to have worked wonderfully well.

ECW: I think it did.

Photo: Rex Walford

*Professor Alice Coleman,
Director of the Second Land
Utilisation Survey, in the
midst of her extensive land-
use map archive, at home*

Chapter 18: The second major land-use survey

Rex Walford in conversation with Professor Alice Coleman

Professor Alice Coleman of Kings College, London, directed a second major Land Utilisation Survey of Britain in the 1960s. Using a more elaborate set of categories than the first Land Utilisation Survey, the Coleman survey replicated total cover of England and Wales and also a large part of Scotland.

Schools and voluntary groups were again recruited to form the bulk of the surveying teams. Although all the field maps were completed, only a small proportion of them (about 100) were reduced to $2^1/_2$-inch scale and published, because of the high costs of colour map printing and the difficulty of obtaining funds at the time. Rex Walford visited Professor Coleman at her home in Dulwich in June 1996 and talked with her about the survey.

RW: How did your involvement with a second national land-use survey begin?

AC: I did not originally intend to do a national survey; it just happened! The GA planned a book series entitled 'Landscapes Through Maps', each based on an Ordnance Survey one-inch sheet, and I wanted to do my home area, the East Kent sheet. An old student, Kenneth Maggs, who also lived in Broadstairs, was interested, and as he was a human geographer while I was then a physical geographer, I thought our collaboration would be a good balance. We also involved members of the Isle of Thanet Geographical Association branch to help, and covered the 500 square miles of the sheet at six-inch scale during a 13-month period in 1958–59.

Using trial and error, we put in some very thorough preparation on the classification, which was more detailed than that of Dudley Stamp's survey, but also fully compatible with it. Kenneth Maggs persuaded me that we should extend the work to the national scale, so we designed a colour scheme for printing at 1:25 000 scale, and investigated costs. We then invited Dudley Stamp to address the Isle of Thanet Geographical Association branch and to advise us on a second Land Utilisation Survey.

We 'mounted' our 99 field maps on the floor of a large school hall, after working furiously to get them all neatly coloured, and hoped Stamp would not notice the few square inches not completed when time ran out. However, he walked round the exhibition and took a great interest. We asked whether we should use the printer who had given us an estimate or approach the Ordnance Survey, to which he replied: 'You won't get the Ordnance Survey to do it. They only did the first survey because there was a war on.' He then astonished us by saying, 'I'll give you £2,000 to get some maps printed.' We wouldn't have dreamed of asking him for money, but he made this offer quite spontaneously.

So between that meeting on 16 October and the end of the year we wrote the Survey Handbook, had it printed and had a 'colourful Christmas', crayoning the centre-page category key in each copy, as we could not afford colour printing. We launched the Survey on 1st January, 1960, at the GA Conference at LSE. The teachers were marvellous. They queued up to colour in on a ten-mile map the 200 square-kilometre areas they were willing to undertake, and bought Handbooks for half-a-crown to give us some initial funding.

In the furious haste to prepare for the launching, I had not formally asked permission of the GA, and in the midst of all the activity the Secretary came and dismantled our exhibit! Since I was a member of the Joint School and taught in LSE, and had Stamp's approval, and had been allocated space by the conference organiser, I did not think I had erred ... The next week I continued the publicity at the IBG Conference at Southampton, where no one demurred and a spirit of academic freedom prevailed. Then I contacted every Director of Education, and they all sent out our letter to their secondary schools, so that by the end of May over 100,000 km^2 had been undertaken – two-thirds of the country. After that it was uphill work to get takers, and I mapped 1500 square miles myself.

RW: Did you find, as the 1996 project has found, that northern Scotland was the most difficult area to get covered?

AC: Stamp advised us to exclude Scotland, but later the Scots became keen so we agreed to cover the lowlands. We even got government money for the surveyors there, unlike those in England. After we had checked the maps and entered corrections I sent them on loan to the National Library of Scotland.

RW: Were your volunteers all teachers and university lecturers?

AC: Teachers, yes, but not a great deal from universities. In the Joint School itself I never drafted students, but had quite a few volunteers. The teachers drew in their pupils, who were very good. It is probably more difficult today, because mapwork has been greatly reduced to make room, first for statistics, and later for computers.

RW: When you set off on this did you have the idea that deliberate comparisons with the first Land Utilisation Survey could be made?

AC: Yes. That is why we used the same basic category colours. We wanted to build on Stamp's foundations. But certain things were bound to be different. For example, in the great Depression of his time, much arable land had 'tumbled down to grass' and so he differentiated rotational ley grass as arable. Christie Willatts told me that the mapping of leys caused the greatest error in the first survey, and a Ministry of Agriculture adviser said that even he could make mistakes when inspecting a field. By then we had mapped over 100 square miles of leys, and decided they could not be distinguished from other grass with any certainty. We therefore included them with grass.

People have said, 'There isn't much difference in the arable cover in the two surveys', and it looks like that on the map, but as a great deal of what we mapped as grass appeared on the earlier maps as arable, the figures are a truer guide, showing a huge arable increase from the 1930s to the 1960s. We developed a very sophisticated computer program to ensure accurate adjustments to give a true statement of change.

RW: You used a more complex set of categories for mapping than Stamp.

AC: Yes. We wanted to make our maps comparable with his but also to record certain things which he could not. For instance, he did not have a category for tended open space, which our later re-surveys have shown to be the fastest growing land use since World War II. He marked roads but not other forms of transport such as airfields, which he had to disguise because they were secret installations in the run-up to World War II. It was quite a challenge to program in subtractions from the uses they were concealed under, but fortunately we had the help of the airfield expert, Dr R. N. E. Blake, who knew individually all the 1,200 airfields there have ever been in the UK.

RW: Did the analysis of a more complex set of categories cause difficulty?

AC: Well, Stamp had seven main categories and we had seventy. He could have seven chapters in a memoir, and write about each with cross-referencing. That was manageable. But I worked out that if you tried to cross-reference even just two uses out of 70, there would be 2,415 possible pairs to relate. So we could not produce County Memoirs like Stamp's.

There were two challenges: to produce statistics and to produce a spatial picture. On the statistical side I worked with the Ordnance Survey's Area Measurement Department. Mr MacKay designed a test map consisting of over 1100 geometrical parcels, which had been measured to the very high accuracy level of 99.3%. We investigated nineteen alternative methods, rating them for accuracy, speed, ease of operation, equipment cost, and, as the project was so large, labour cost. I then invented a new method, systematic point sampling, which was the fastest, while also being highly accurate and economical, and did not require expensive equipment. It was exhaustively applied to the test map in 300 trials by Mrs Enid Wilkinson, to ascertain the best point density. The national measurement took eight man-years.

This methodology was published by the GA. The 1996 survey is using the *theory* of our technique but is not quite so streamlined in practice.

Stamp had an excellent slogan, 'Facts on the Map', which is essential for all geographers. With 70 categories, however, the detail of the facts becomes very complex, and I coined a companion slogan: 'Patterns on the Map'. This was our other challenge: cartographic analysis. Essentially, it was a classification of land-use mixtures. These were compatible mixtures which we called townscape, farmscape and wildscape, and incompatible mixtures: urban fringe and marginal fringe. It contrasted with the then prevalent reliance on grid squares, as I wanted to show actual, visible boundaries for easy map-reading. We did use grid squares as an initial aid in an iteration procedure to work out the methodology. The GA published my paper on the initial concept of scape and fringe territories after I had applied it broadly to 1300 square miles of Canada. Later we analysed, or rather synthesised, the whole of England and Wales in detail. The resulting map proved objective in two ways. Operationally, different operators would independently create the same boundaries to the nearest millimetre, and in real-world terms, visiting strangers recognised the patterns of their home areas as a true reflection of what existed. This national map is now on sale.

RW: Did you complete the survey just with volunteers?

AC: Almost, but at the end the Department of the Environment funded half-a-dozen people to fill the gaps in England. This was particularly valuable for checking queries on volunteers' maps, especially the vegetation which was the hardest to survey. No funds were available for Wales and I had to meet that cost personally.

RW: Did you ever meet or go out with the survey volunteers?

AC: Yes. I set up meetings around the country to spend half-days with groups of volunteers. However, most teachers felt that the Handbook was a sufficient guide. We had prepared it with very clear text and illustrations, and it was small enough to roll up in a pocket to take in the field.

I've looked at your beautifully produced 1996 Survey Pack, but wonder whether perhaps some of the loose leaves might get lost?

RW: We had a lot of discussion about what precise format the 1996 survey instructions should take. There are things for and against a loose-leaf format. But we wanted to make sheets easily accessible for photocopying.

AC: Of course. We were working before the days of universal photocopying. We just said 'Buy the handbook and buy the maps.'

RW: I know that although you have all the field maps, printed maps are available only for certain parts of the country because of the difficulties of getting finance for the great costs involved in producing the colour maps. Did you ever produce definitive versions of national, regional or local statistics, though?

AC: National and county figures, yes. And the county statistics could be combined to give regional figures. We also produced quite a few local figures for special purposes such as river-authority catchments, housing estates, and public-enquiry areas. I published a 26,000-word summary analysis as a special issue of *The Architects' Journal* (19 January 1977). I was told that Prince Philip rang them up and said 'Send me two more copies for my friends.' They did not even realise he was a reader.

I was pleased with that article because they printed full-colour maps showing the scapes and fringes, and there were also many photographs. The editor said to me, 'We hesitate to ask you to do this because we know you'll be wanting to write a book', but I replied, 'I'd like to do it because it would be a good way of working out a skeleton for the book.' But so many things have cropped up since that I am only now writing the 'Land-Use Strategy' book.

RW: So seventeen years afterwards the results of the survey were still bearing fruit?

AC: Well, Stamp took seventeen years before he produced his book. He started in 1930 and published in 1947. We started in 1960 and published in 1977. He said he had half the country finished by 1933. We had half the country finished by 1963. So we followed very much in his footsteps, although I could not get the government support that he did because, thankfully, there was no war to stimulate it. Nor could I get people to write county memoirs, because the more detailed analysis could not be made quick and simple. And, of course, the second survey continued to bear fruit long after then. I was asked to testify in many public enquiries and planning appeals, and we almost always won because I could produce the hard facts on the maps and patterns on the map.

RW: Did you do all this for its own sake or was there a subtext? How post-war planning controls had affected the landscape, for instance?

AC: For its own sake. We were interested in land use for the sake of land use. At first it was purely academic curiosity. I expected to find much more prosperous farming than in the 1930s, and this proved to be the case. But I also expected to find planning improvements and in many cases the reverse had happened.

RW: What would your advice be to those involved in a 1996 survey?

AC: In many ways you have advantages, because you've seen to it that you have a lot of people on your side. I was only a young lecturer when I started the second Land Utilisation Survey and did not have the same wide range of contacts. If I had been asked for advice before you made the decisions I would have said 'Keep your classification compatible with ours, even though it is simpler, and choose your sample areas on the basis of our scape and fringe map, rather than in relation to a non-land-use distribution.'

Land use is the real central basis of geography. I've had to include vegetation surveys, inner-city surveys, farming surveys, graffiti surveys – all sorts of things in the course of this work. It brings all the aspects together. Students often say, 'Geography is integrated', but their course may be so specialised that when they are asked to produce an integrated view, they do not really know what it means. But land use is an excellent example of the integrating potential of geography.

Appendix 1:
The survey categories

This appendix is a (slightly edited) extract from the material provided in the Survey Handbook which was issued to all survey teams who registered with Land Use – UK.

There is no single land-use classification that is accepted by everybody. What does exist is a variety of different systems that have been devised for a variety of different purposes by academics, planners, government officials and others. These systems vary according to the purpose for which they are used, the scale of coverage, the method of gathering the information and so on. It is also the case that, over a period of years, some of the approaches have had to change to take account of new land uses or changing concerns.

The system being used for this survey is a variant of the 1994 'baseline classification' developed by the Institute of Terrestrial Ecology (ITE) – but there are two important amendments. Firstly, it has been simplified to make it more user-friendly. Secondly (and importantly) the ITE classification is especially concerned with rural land, and so we have expanded the urban categories. After all, almost 90% of the population of the UK lives in towns and cities, and their day-to-day experience is dominated by urban land uses.

The scheme of classification and the map-colouring procedure suggested means that it should be possible to make approximate visual comparisons with the published maps of the second Land Utilisation Survey of the 1960s.

The main categories of classification are listed below:

1	arable land	brown
2	horticulture, orchards, vineyards and soft fruit	magenta
3	grass	yellow-green
4	heathland and bog	laser lemon
5	woodland and shrub	green
6	inland rocks and scree	pink
7	wetland and water	sky blue
8	coastal features	blue
9	quarries and other extractive industries	wild watermelon
10	agricultural buildings	violet
11	transport routes and features	orange
12	residential	black
13	commercial and business uses	grey/atomic tangerine
14	industrial premises and utilities	red
15	public institutions	maroon
16	tended open space	aqua green
17	derelict and waste land, and buildings	shocking pink
18	land in transition	green-blue
19	unsurveyed	white
20	sea (this category was added at a later stage)	

In the remainder of this appendix, the survey categories are explained and amplified.

1 Arable land

This includes all land which, in the year of survey, has been tilled/ploughed for agricultural crops (including *wheat, barley, oats, sugar-beet, turnips/swedes/other root crops, kale, potatoes, field beans, field peas, maize, rye, oilseed rape*, and 'new' crops such as *linseed, evening primrose* and *lupins*). But **beware** potential confusion with recently-sown grass (see 3 Grass) and small fields (plots) of vegetables (see 2 Horticulture). *Setaside land* (which is land taken out of agriculture on a temporary basis and which can be recognised by the large variety of weeds or by dead vegetation, following spraying) should be included here. *Setaside should be specially noted as part of Task 2.*

2 Horticulture, orchards, vineyards and soft fruit

Horticulture is 'gardening on a large scale', and typically includes mixtures of vegetable crops within one field or plot. This may be for commercial or domestic purposes but it should not include allotments or gardens (see **12** Residential).

Orchards, in this context, are those which are managed commercially to produce *apples, pears, plums* and *other tree-borne fruits. Hop-orchards* should also be included here. But it should not include, for example, a small number of apple trees at the bottom of a garden (see **12** Residential).

Although they are rare, there is a chance that, in the southern half of England, you may record a *vineyard*.

Soft fruit includes *strawberry and raspberry fields* and other 'berry-fruits' grown for commercial purposes, including 'Pick-Your-Own' locations.

3 Grass

This includes all land where grass species form the dominant land cover (including *meadow, pasture, upland grass* and *moorland grass*.

There are two major problem areas: (1) recently-sown grass in fields (i.e. lots of bare soil between the plants) can look like an arable crop – ask the farmer if you are unsure; (2) in the uplands there are mixtures of grassland, heathland and bog (see **4** Heathland and bog) which are difficult to map separately. Try to identify which species dominates and map accordingly.

Areas of *field rushes and bracken* should also be included in this category (because, with suitable management, grassland could be re-established).

4 Heathland and bog

Heathland is characteristically dominated by heather and other small woody shrubs. It occurs in the uplands (moorland) and lowlands (lowland heaths) and is often mixed with bogs and grassland. Try to identify areas of land which are dominated by heather for this category, and separate them from land which might otherwise be recorded as grassland (see category **3**).

Bog includes wet spongy land, usually on peat, and often in the uplands in the north and west of Britain. It does not include *marshes* and *fens* which tend to occur in lowland situations on mineral soils (see **7** Wetland and water).

5 Woodland and shrub

This category covers all land where *trees, shrubs* and *bushes* are dominant (i.e. they cover more than 50% of the area being mapped). A handful of bushes in a field would not count as woodland, unless they were close together and could be recorded sensibly as a visibly separate area on the map. *All features which are enclosed within a wood* (such as fire-breaks, woodland rides, glades and felled areas) should be recorded here.

6 Inland rocks and scree

This includes all *bare rock* (usually in the uplands, but also including unvegetated limestone pavement) and *screes* where there is little or no vegetation cover (e.g. moss-covered boulders). It would include *cliffs on mountains* but not at the coast (see **8** Coastal features). NB Be careful not to exaggerate the extent of cliffs on your map.

7 Wetland and water

This includes all inland water (*lakes, ponds, reservoirs, rivers, canals* and *streams*) which are large enough to be mapped at 1:10 000 scale. It also includes vegetation types/habitats where some standing water is likely to be visible for most of the year (e.g. marshes and fens, but see also **4** Heathland and bog). Where rivers meet the coast (estuaries), the main high-water mark, as shown on OS maps, should be used to distinguish rivers from estuarine sea.

8 Coastal features

This category includes sandy features (such as *dunes, beaches, bars, spits*), gravel and pebble shores, rock and cliffs. It also includes bare and vegetated mud at the coast, e.g. salt marsh. Maritime grassland (e.g. on cliff tops) should be recorded as **3** Grass.

9 Quarries and other extractive industries

This includes all types of *quarries*, including open-cast coal mines, and their *associated buildings and machinery*. Old mine-workings which have been revegetated should be recorded under their current land-cover type.

10 Agricultural buildings

This includes all of the built environment to do with agriculture such as *out-buildings, barns, stables, yards, pens* and *sheep-folds*, but not farmhouses, which may well be occupied by people unconnected with the agricultural industry. Farmhouses should be recorded under **12** Residential.

11 Transport routes and features

This includes all *through roads*, but not most roads in housing or industrial estates or in the grounds of large institutions. These latter should be classified as residential, industrial etc. as appropriate. *Motorways, their verges and their service-stations* should be included, as should *petrol filling-stations* on through routes.

Also include *railways*, including sidings, and marshalling yards, *canals, airfields, port facilities* and *marinas* and their associated buildings (e.g. railway stations, port offices, airport terminals).

Public coach and car parks should be included, but not car parks attached to schools, hospitals, factories, etc., which should be classified accordingly.

12 Residential

This includes *houses, flats, and adjoining garages, gardens, estate roads, paths* etc. (New housing areas may need to be added to the map.) Also include *residential caravan parks, chalets*, etc., *farmhouses* (see **10**), and allotments because they are functionally associated with residential development.

13 Commercial and business uses

This includes *offices* and financial services, banks, building societies, estate agents, surveyors, solicitors, etc., and *shops* selling goods or services, including hairdressers, builders' merchants, garages, etc., and *street markets*.

It also includes *public houses, restaurants, hotels*, and indoor sports and entertainment venues such as *cinemas, swimming pools, bingo halls* and *amusement arcades*. Also, *wholesale and warehouse buildings, stockyards, cattle-markets, scrap and timber yards, cash-and-carry outlets*, and *cold stores*.

14 Industrial premises and utilities

This category should include all kinds of *factory buildings* and their installations, *refineries, ship-building yards, mills, breweries, dairies, cement works*, etc. Also include the associated space around them used for parking, deliveries, etc.

Utilities should also be included, such as sewage-farms, power-stations, electricity transformers, telephone exchanges, transmission masts and aerials, incinerators, gasworks, covered reservoirs, and crematoria (though not cemeteries – see **16**)

15 Public institutions

This includes *government offices*, town halls, police stations, post offices, law courts, prisons and fire stations, and the associated space around them.

But it also includes (using a wider definition of 'public') *schools*, colleges, universities, training establishments, etc., *churches and chapels, museums, art galleries, exhibition halls, large houses open to the public* (together with their grounds, if not farmed actively).

Health and medical services such as hospitals, clinics, nursing homes, convalescent homes and geriatric homes should also be included.

16 Tended open space

Within this category should be included *public parks and gardens, playing-fields and playgrounds, football, rugby, hockey and cricket pitches, golf courses*, etc., and *cemeteries*. It should also include informal areas, if they show evidence of being 'managed' for recreational purposes.

17 Derelict and waste land, and buildings

This should include land and buildings (most probably found within urban areas) which have no present or imminent formal use. Some such land or buildings may have had a recent use which has been abandoned. Other sites may appear to have been vacant or wasteland for a longer period.

18 Land in transition

This should include construction sites, earth-moving sites, and landfill areas.

19 Unsurveyed

Very occasionally, it may prove impossible to survey some areas due to lack of access etc. – but we hope this will be a very rare event. (It proved to be so – only 0.5% fell into this category.)

20 Sea

Because the Ordnance Survey grid does not take account of the coastline, some grid squares consisted partly of sea, rather than land. At a late stage survey teams were instructed to use the vacant 20th category for these areas of sea on their maps, and to distinguish it carefully from categories **7** and **8**.

Appendix 2: The surveyors

Schools and other institutions which returned Land Use – UK results

Abbey School, Tewkesbury, Gloucestershire

Abergwili VC Primary School, Carmarthen, Dyfed

Aboyne Lodge JMI and N School, St Albans, Hertfordshire

Acomb Primary School, York

ADT College, London SW15

Aireville School, Skipton, North Yorkshire

Albrighton County Junior School, Albrighton, West Midlands

Albyn School for Girls, Aberdeen

Alderman Newton's School, Leicester

Alexandra Junior School, Normacot, Staffordshire

Alford Academy, Alford, Aberdeenshire

All Saints RC School, Sheffield, South Yorkshire

All Saints School, Cockermouth, Cumbria

Alleyne's High School, Stone, Staffordshire

Alleyn's School, Dulwich, London SE22

Allonby Primary School, Maryport, Cumbria

Alltwalis Primary School, Alltwalis, Carmarthen, Dyfed

Alsager High School and Cranberry Juniors, Alsager, Cheshire

Altwood School, Maidenhead, Berkshire

Andover CE Primary School, Andover, Hampshire

Antrobus Women's Institute, Nr Northwich, Cheshire

Archers Court School, Whitfield, Kent

Armathwaite School, Armathwaite, Cumbria

Arnett Hills JMI School, Rickmansworth, Hertfordshire

Arran High School, Lamlash, Isle of Arran

Arthur Mellows Village College, Glinton, Cambridgeshire

Ashcroft High School, Luton, Bedfordshire

Ashford School (Junior School), Ashford, Kent

Ashlands First School, Ilkley, West Yorkshire

Ashmead School, Reading, Berkshire

Ashton on Mersey School, Sale, Greater Manchester

Aston Comprehensive, Swallownest, South Yorkshire

Auchinleck Academy, Auchinleck, Ayrshire

Axton Chase School, Longfield, Kent

Aylesbury High School, Aylesbury, Buckinghamshire

Aylestone School, Hereford

Ayr Academy, Ayr

Balfron High School, Balfron, Glasgow

Ballymena Academy, Ballymena, County Antrim

Bampton Endowed School, Nr Penrith, Cumbria

Bannockburn High School, Bannockburn, Stirlingshire

Bardney Primary School, Bardney, Lincolnshire

Barkerend First School, Bradford, West Yorkshire

Barking Abbey Comprehensive School, Barking, Essex

Barr Beacon Community School, Nr Walsall, West Midlands

Barrow Grove Junior School, Sittingbourne, Kent

Baschurch CE Primary School, Baschurch, Shropshire

Batley Grammar School, Batley, West Yorkshire

Bawdsey VC Primary School, Bawdsey, Suffolk

Bawtry Mayflower J and I School, Bawtry, South Yorkshire

Bay House School, Gosport, Hampshire

Beaminster Comprehensive, Beaminster, Dorset

Beardwood School, Blackburn, Lancashire

Bebside Middle School, Blyth, Northumberland

Bedford Modern School, Bedford

Beech Hyde JMI School, Wheathampstead, Hertfordshire

Beechfield JMI School, Watford, Hertfordshire

Beechlawn School (Special), Hillsborough, County Down

Beechwood County Primary School, Runcorn, Cheshire

Beehive Lane County Primary School, Chelmsford, Essex

Belfast High School, Newtownabbey, County Antrim

Belfast Royal Academy, Belfast

Belgrave High School, Tamworth, Staffordshire

Belle Vue Girls' School, Bradford, West Yorkshire

Belle Vue Primary School, Wordsley, West Midlands

Bellfield Primary School, Hull, East Yorkshire

Belsay County First School, Newcastle upon Tyne

Belvue School, Northolt, Middlesex

Benfield County Junior School, Portslade, East Sussex

Benington JMI School, Benington, Hertfordshire

Bentham School, Bentham, Nr Lancaster

Benton Park School, Rawdon, West Yorkshire

Berkhamsted Schools, Berkhamsted, Hertfordshire

Berry Hill High School, Bucknall, Staffordshire

Berwick High School, Berwick upon Tweed, Northumberland

Beulah County Primary School, Newcastle Emlyn, Dyfed

Bexhill High School, Bexhill, East Sussex

Beyton Middle School, Beyton, Suffolk

Bickerton CE Primary, Malpas, Cheshire

Biddick School, Washington, Tyne and Wear

Biddulph High School, Knypersley, Staffordshire

Bignold Middle School, Norwich, Norfolk

Bingley Grammar School, Bingley, West Yorkshire

Birkenhead Sixth Form College, Birkenhead, Merseyside

Bishop Heber High School, Malpas, Cheshire

Bishop Stopford School, Kettering, Northamptonshire

Bishop Vesey's Grammar School, Sutton Coldfield, West Midlands

Bishops' High School, Boughton, Cheshire

Blairgowrie High School, Blairgowrie, Tayside

Blanford Mere Primary School, Kingswinford, West Midlands

Blencathra Centre, The Field Studies Council, Threlkeld, Cumbria

Blyth Tynedale High School, Blyth, Northumberland

Blythe Bridge High School, Stoke on Trent, Staffordshire

Boclair Academy, Bearsden, Glasgow

Bodiam Primary School, Robertsbridge, East Sussex

Bollinbrook CE Primary School, Macclesfield, Cheshire

Bolton School (Boys' Division, Junior Dept), Bolton, Greater Manchester

Boney Hay Primary School, Walsall, West Midlands

Boroughmuir High School, Edinburgh

Boundstone Community College, Lancing, West Sussex

Bournemouth School for Boys, Bournemouth, Dorset

Bournemouth School for Girls, Bournemouth, Dorset

Bournville School, Birmingham, West Midlands

Braeside School, Buckhurst Hill, Essex

Brampton Primary School, Bexleyheath, Kent

Braunton School and College, Nr Barnstaple, Devon

Brechfa County Primary School, Brechfa, Dyfed

Brechin High School, Brechin, Angus

Brent Inspection Service, Centre For Staff Development, London NW10

Brentside Primary School Road, Hanwell, London W7

Brewood CE Middle School, Brewood, Staffordshire

Brierton Comprehensive School, Hartlepool, Cleveland

Bristol Cathedral School, Bristol, Avon

Bristol Grammar School, Bristol, Avon

Bromley High School, Bromley, Kent

Brompton–Westbrook CP School, Gillingham, Kent

Brookfield High School, Kirkby, Merseyside

Broomfield School, Southgate, London N14

Buckhaven High School, Buckhaven, Fife

Buckie Community High School, Buckie, Banffshire

Burnsall VA Primary School, Burnsall, North Yorkshire

Bushey Hall School, Bushey, Hertfordshire

Buttershaw Upper School, Bradford, West Yorkshire

Caio County Primary School, Pumsaint, Dyfed

Caister High School, Caister on Sea, Norfolk

Caistor Grammar School, Caistor, Lincolnshire

Calday Grange Grammar School, West Kirby, Merseyside

Cambridge University, Department of Education, Cambridge

Cannock Chase High School, Cannock, Staffordshire

Cantell School, Bassett, Southampton

Canterbury Christ Church College, Canterbury, Kent

Capel Iwan County Primary School, Newcastle Emlyn, Dyfed

Carbeile Junior School, Torpoint, Cornwall

Cardinal Heenan High School, Liverpool, Merseyside

Carlton Road Primary School, Boston, Lincolnshire

Carnoustie High School, Carnoustie, Angus

Cartmel CE Primary School, Cartmel, Cumbria

Casterton Community College, Great Casterton, Lincolnshire

Castle School, Thornbury, Bristol, Avon

Chadsmoor Junior CE School, Chadsmoor, Staffordshire

Chalford Hill County Primary School, Stroud, Gloucestershire

Chambersbury JMI School, Hemel Hempstead, Hertfordshire

Channing School, Highgate, London N6

Charles Dickens School, Broadstairs, Kent

Charterhouse School, Godalming, Surrey

Chase Bridge Primary School, Twickenham, Middlesex

Chase High School, Malvern, Hereford and Worcester

Chase Terrace Primary School, Chase Terrace, Staffordshire

Chatton CE First School, Chatton, Northumberland

Chaulden JM School, Hemel Hampstead, Hertfordshire

Cheam High School, Cheam, Surrey

Chelmer Valley High School, Broomfield, Chelmsford, Essex

Cheltenham and Gloucester College, Cheltenham, Gloucestershire

Chepstow Comprehensive School, Chepstow, Gwent

Chetham's School of Music, Manchester

Childer Thornton CP School, Childer Thornton, Cheshire

Chilwell Comprehensive School, Beeston, Nottinghamshire

Chingford Junior School, Castle Hedingham, Essex

Chingford School, Nevin Drive, London E4

Christow Primary School, Exeter, Devon

Church Eaton Primary School, Church Eaton, Staffordshire

Churchfield School, London SE2

City of Birmingham Tuition Service, Birmingham, West Midlands

Cleeve School, Bishop's Cleeve, Gloucestershire

Cliffe House Field Centre, Shepley, West Yorkshire

Clinton Park County Primary School, Tattershall, Lincolnshire

Clitheroe Royal Grammar School, Clitheroe, Lancashire

Clough Head Primary School, Golcar, West Yorkshire

Clutton Primary School, Nr Tattenhall, Cheshire

Coates Primary School, Peterborough, Cambridgeshire

Codsall Middle School, Wolverhampton, West Midlands

Colbayns High School, Clacton on Sea, Essex

Collegiate High School, Blackpool, Lancashire

Colston's Girls' School, Bristol, Avon

Combe CE Primary School, Witney, Oxfordshire

Comberton Middle School, Borrington Road, Kidderminster, Hereford and Worcester

Connaught School for Girls, London E11

Conway Centre, Llanfairpwllgwyn, Anglesey, Gwynedd

Coombe Girls' School, New Malden, Surrey

Cooper Perry Primary School, Seighford, Staffordshire

Coopers Company and Coburn School, Upminster, Essex

Coundon Court School, Coventry, West Midlands

Court Lodge School, Horley, Surrey

Cowbridge School, Cowbridge, South Glamorgan

Cowplain School, Waterlooville, Hampshire

Cranborne Middle School, Nr Wimborne, Dorset

Cressbrook Primary School, Nr Buxton, Derbyshire

Crown Hills Community College, Leicester

Crown Woods School, London SE9

Cuddington School, Nr Aylesbury, Buckinghamshire

Cumbernauld High School, Cumbernauld, Dumbartonshire

Cumnock Academy, Cumnock, Ayrshire

Dartford Girls' Grammar School, Dartford, Kent

Dean CE Primary School, Workington, Cumbria

Dean Close School, Cheltenham, Gloucestershire

Deepings School, Deeping St James, Cambridgeshire
Delaval Middle School, Blyth, Northumberland
Denes High School, Lowestoft, Suffolk
Dennington Primary School, Nr Woodbridge, Suffolk
Dent CE Primary School, Dent, Cumbria
Denton CP School, Nr Newhaven, East Sussex
Derrymont School, Arnold, Nottingham
Derwent Community Primary School, Derby
Derwent Vale Primary School, Workington, Cumbria
d'Hautree School, Jersey, Channel Isles
Didcot Girls' School, Didcot, Oxfordshire
Dinnington Comprehensive, Dinnington, South Yorkshire
Dinting CE VA Primary School, Glossop, Derbyshire
Ditcham Park School, Petersfield, Hampshire
Ditton CE Primary School, Widnes, Cheshire
Dixie Grammar School, Market Bosworth, Leicestershire
Dorchester Primary School, Worcester Park, Surrey
Douglas Ewart High School, Newton Stewart,
    Wigtownshire
Dowdales School, Dalton in Furness, Cumbria
Dragon School, Oxford
Duchess's High School, Alnwick, Northumberland
Dunblane High School, Dunblane, Perthshire
Dyce Academy, Dyce, Aberdeenshire
Eaglesfield School, Woolwich, London SE18
Eagleswell Junior School, Llantwit Major, South
    Glamorgan
Easingwold School, Easingwold, North Yorkshire
East Barnet School, New Barnet, Hertfordshire
East Bergholt High School, Colchester, Essex
East London EO Group, Walthamstow, London E17
East Preston Junior School, East Preston, West Sussex
Eastcroft Primary School, Kirkby, Merseyside
Easthampstead Park School, Bracknell, Berkshire
Eastover Primary School, Bridgewater, Somerset
Edgehill College, Bideford, Devon
Elgin Academy, Elgin, Morayshire
Elizabeth College, St Peter Port, Guernsey, Channel Isles
Ellesmere College, Ellesmere, Shropshire
Ellon Academy, Ellon, Aberdeenshire
Embley Park School, Romsey, Hampshire
Emerson Park School, Hornchurch, Essex
Endon High School, Stoke on Trent, Staffordshire
Ennerdale and Kinniside Primary School, Cleator,
    Cumbria
Epsom College, Epsom, Surrey
Erith School, Erith, Kent
Ermysted's Grammar School, Skipton, North Yorkshire
Estover Community College, Plymouth, Devon
Eyrescroft Primary School, Bretton, Peterborough,
    Cambridgeshire
Faber RC Primary School, Oakamoor, Staffordshire
Fairfield High School, Peterchurch, Hereford and
    Worcester
Falmer School, Brighton, East Sussex
Farr Secondary School, Bettyhill, Caithness
Featherstone High School, Southall, Middlesex
Felsted School, Dunmow, Essex
Feltonfleet School, Cobham, Surrey

Ffarmers School, Llanwida, Carmarthen, Dyfed
Ffynone House School, Swansea, West Glamorgan
Finham Park School, Coventry, West Midlands
Finningley CE School, Doncaster, South Yorkshire
Firrhill High School, Edinburgh
Fitzalan High School, Leckwith, Cardiff
Fitzwimarc School, Rayleigh, Essex
Flax Hill Junior School, Gillway, Staffordshire
Flexlands School, Chobham, Surrey
Forest Park Primary School, Nr Hawley, Staffordshire
Foula Primary School, Foula, Shetland
Friends School, Saffron Walden, Essex
Frithville County Primary School, Boston, Lincolnshire
Frome Community College, Frome, Somerset
Gisleham Middle School, Carlton Colville, Suffolk
Gledhow Primary School, Leeds, West Yorkshire
Glen Urquhart High School, Drumnadrochit, Inverness
Globe Primary School, Bethnal Green, London E2
Glyn Derw High School, Ely, Cardiff
Godolphin School, Salisbury, Wiltshire
Golden Hillock Community School, Sparkhill,
    Birmingham, West Midlands
Gorsey Bank County Primary School, Wilmslow, Cheshire
Grange Junior School, Runcorn, Cheshire
Great Abington Primary School, Great Abington,
    Cambridge
Great Cornard Upper School, Great Cornard, Suffolk
Great Linford Combined School, Great Linford,
    Buckinghamshire
Greenhead CE First School, Nr Carlisle, Cumbria
Greenhead Grammar School, Keighley, West Yorkshire
Greenlands High School, Bispham, Lancashire
Greenock Academy, Greenock, Renfrewshire
Greenslade Primary School, Plumstead Common, London
    SE18
Grove Junior School, Northwood, Stoke on Trent,
    Staffordshire
Guide Post Middle School, Choppington, Northumberland
Guildford High School, Guildford, Surrey
Gumley House School, Isleworth, Middlesex
Gwynedd County Primary School, Flint, Clwyd
Haberdashers' Aske's School for Girls, Elstree,
    Hertfordshire
Hagley Park High School, Rugeley, Staffordshire
Halesbury School, Halesowen, West Midlands
Hammond School, Chester
Hamond's High School, Swaffham, Norfolk
Hampshire Outdoor Centre, Portsmouth, Hampshire
Hampton School, Hampton, Middlesex
Handsworth Grammar School, Birmingham, West
    Midlands
Hanover Primary School, London N1
Harefield Junior School, Harefield, Middlesex
Harrogate Grammar School, Harrogate, North Yorkshire
Harthill County Primary School, Tattenhall, Cheshire
Hartley County Primary School, Hartley, Kent
Harvington School, Ealing, London W5
Helenswood School, Hastings, East Sussex
Helsby High School, Helsby, Cheshire

Helston School, Helston, Cornwall

Hempstead CE Primary School, Hempstead, Gloucestershire

Hemsworth High School, Hemsworth, West Yorkshire

Henry Cort School, Fareham, Hampshire

Hereford Cathedral School, Hereford

Herne Junior School, Crowborough, East Sussex

Heron Cross Primary School, Fenton, Staffordshire

Heron Hill School, Kendal, Cumbria

Hexham Middle School, Hexham, Northumberland

Highworth Grammar School For Girls, Ashford, Kent

Hillcrest School, Hastings, East Sussex

Hinchingbrooke School, Huntingdon, Cambridgeshire

Hind Leys Community College, Shepshed, Leicestershire

Hinde House School, Sheffield, South Yorkshire

Hirst High School, Ashington, Northumberland

Hitchin Boys' School, Hitchin, Hertfordshire

Hitchin Girls' School, Hitchin, Hertfordshire

Hollesley County Primary School, Hollesley, Suffolk

Hollins County High School, Accrington, Lancashire

Hollinsclough Primary School, Nr Longnor, Derbyshire

Holy Trinity Junior School, Halifax, West Yorkshire

Holy Trinity School, Gossops Green, West Sussex

Honeyhill Primary School, Paston, Peterborough, Cambridgeshire

Honley High School, Honley, West Yorkshire

Honywood School, Coggeshall, Essex

Hook CE Primary School, Goole, East Yorkshire

Hope Primary School, Hope, Derbyshire

Horn Park Primary School, Lee, London SE12

Horndean Community School, Waterlooville, Hampshire

Horringer Court Middle School, Bury St Edmunds, Suffolk

Horton Kirby CE Primary School, Dartford, Kent

Hove Park School, Hove, East Sussex

Howard County Primary School, Tamworth, Staffordshire

Howard of Effingham School, Effingham, Surrey

Huddersfield University, Huddersfield, West Yorkshire

Hugh Christie Technology Centre, Tonbridge, Kent

Huish Episcopi School, Langport, Somerset

Hulme Grammar School for Boys, Oldham, Greater Manchester

Hurst Green CE School, Hurst Green, East Sussex

Hurst Primary School, Bexley, Kent

Hymers College, Hull, East Yorkshire

Idsall School, Shifnal, Shropshire

Ipswich High School, Ipswich, Suffolk

Islay High School, Bowmore, Isle Of Islay

Ivanhoe High School and Commercial College, Ashby de la Zouch, Leicestershire

Ivegill CE Primary School, Ivegill, Cumbria

Jaffray School, Erdington, Birmingham, West Midlands

John Leggott Sixth Form College, Scunthorpe, Lincolnshire

John Mason School, Abingdon, Oxfordshire

John of Gaunt School, Trowbridge, Wiltshire

John Paxton CJ School, Sawston, Cambridge

John Taylor High School, Barton Under Needwood, Staffordshire

Joiners Square Primary School, Hanley, Staffordshire

Jordanhill School, Glasgow

Juniper Hall Field Centre, Mickleham, Surrey

Keble School, Winchmore Hill, London N21

Keith Grammar School, Keith, Banffshire

Kesgrave High School, Kesgrave, Suffolk

Kesteven and Sleaford High School, Sleaford, Lincolnshire

Kilquhanity House School, Castle Douglas, Kirkcudbrightshire

Kimbolton St James' CE Primary, Kimbolton, Herefordshire

King Alfred School, London NW11

King Edward VI College, Totnes, Devon

King Edward VI Handsworth School, Handsworth, Birmingham, West Midlands

King Edward VI School, Lichfield, Staffordshire

King Edward VI School, Morpeth, Northumberland

King Edward VI School, Retford, Nottinghamshire

King Edward VII High School, Kings Lynn, Norfolk

King Edward's School, Bath, Avon

Kings Court Preparatory School, Catherington, Hampshire

Kingsdown School, Stratton St Margaret, Wiltshire

Kingsholm CE Primary School, Gloucester

Kingsmead High School, Hednesford, Staffordshire

Kingussie High School, Kingussie, Inverness

Kirkby Thore School, Nr Penrith, Cumbria

Kirkcudbright Academy, Kirkcudbright

Kirkoswald CE School, Kirkoswald, Cumbria

Knights Templar School, Baldock, Hertfordshire

Kyle Academy, Ayr

Lamplugh School, Frizington, Cumbria

Lancaster Boys School, Leicester

Landau Forte College, Derby

Langholm Academy, Langholm, Dumfriesshire

Langley Education Centre, Langley, Cheshire

Larne Grammar School, Larne, County Antrim

Le Rocquier School, St Clement, Jersey

Lea Valley High School, Enfield, Middlesex

Leek High School, Leek, Staffordshire

Leventhorpe School, Sawbridgeworth, Hertfordshire

Lewes Old Grammar School, Lewes, East Sussex

Light Hall School, Shirley, West Midlands

Lincolnshire Geographical Association, Lincoln

Little Aston JM and I School, Sutton Coldfield, West Midlands

Little Green JM School, Croxley Green, Hertfordshire

Liverpool Hope University College, Liverpool, Merseyside

Llangadog County Primary School, Llangadog, Carmarthen, Dyfed

Llanidloes County Primary School, Llanidloes, Powys

Llanrug Outdoor Education Centre, Caernarfon, Gwynedd

Llansadwrn County Primary School, Llanwrda, Camarthen, Dyfed

Llanycrwys County Primary School, Llanwrda, Camarthen, Dyfed

Loders Primary School, Bridport, Dorset

Lomond School, Helensburgh, Dumbartonshire

Long Marton School, Nr Appleby, Cumbria

Longbenton Community College, Longbenton, Tyne and Wear

Longfields County Primary School, Bicester, Oxfordshire

Longparish CE Primary School, Nr Andover, Hampshire

Lord Wandsworth College, Long Sutton, Hampshire

Lord Williams's School, Thame, Oxfordshire

Lordship Farm JMI School, Letchworth, Hertfordshire

Loughborough High School, Loughborough, Leicestershire

Luckley Oakfield School, Wokingham, Berkshire

Ludlow School, Burway, Ludlow, Shropshire

Lunnasting Primary School, Vidlin, Shetland

Lymm High School, Lymm, Cheshire

Mackie Academy, Stonehaven, Kincardineshire

Macmillan College, Middlesbrough, Cleveland

Madresfield CE Primary School, Madresfield, Hereford and Worcester

Maengwynedd Outdoor Education Centre, Nr Oswestry, Shropshire

Malcolm Sargeant School, Stamford, Lincolnshire

Malpas Alport Primary School, Malpas, Cheshire

Malton School, Malton, North Yorkshire

Manchester Grammar School, Manchester

Manchester High School for Girls, Rusholme, Manchester

Manor County Primary School, Drayton Bassett, Staffordshire

Manor Park County Primary School, Knutsford, Cheshire

Manshead School, Caddington, Bedfordshire

Marham First and Middle School, Marham, Norfolk

Mark Rutherford School, Bedford

Marlborough College, Marlborough, Wiltshire

Meadowdale Middle School, Bedlington, Northumberland

Meadows Community School, Whittington, Derbyshire

Medina Valley Centre, Newport, Isle of Wight

Merchant Taylors' School, Northwood, Middlesex

Merdon Junior School, Chandler's Ford, Hampshire

Meridian School, Royston, Hertfordshire

Merlyn Rees High School, Leeds, West Yorkshire

Mid Kent College, Maidstone, Kent

Middleton Technology School, Middleton, Manchester

Midhurst Grammar School, Midhurst, West Sussex

Mildenhall Upper School, Mildenhall, Suffolk

Millfield Junior School, Glastonbury, Somerset

Millom School, Millom, Cumbria

Milton Mount First and Middle School, Crawley, West Sussex

Minster School, York

Moat Hall Primary School, Great Wyrley, Staffordshire

Monks Coppenhall County Primary School, Crewe, Cheshire

Monk's Walk School, Welwyn Garden City, Hertfordshire

Moorside High School, Werrington, Staffordshire

Morrison's Academy, Crieff, Perthshire

Morton CE Primary School, Bourne, Lincolnshire

Mount CE Primary School, Newark, Nottinghamshire

Mount House School, Tavistock, Devon

Mowbray County Junior School, South Shields, Tyne and Wear

Nantgaredig County Primary School, Nantgaredig, Carmarthen, Dyfed

Navenby CE Primary School, Navenby, Lincolnshire

Nelson and Colne College, Nelson, Lancashire

Netherhall School, Cambridge

New Hall Preparatory School, Chelmsford, Essex

New Hall School, Chelmsford, Essex

New Haw Junior School, Addlestone, Surrey

New Leake County Primary School, New Leake, Lincolnshire

Newport Free Grammar School, Newport, Essex

Normanby County Primary School, Normanby by Spital, Lincolnshire

North Berwick High School, North Berwick, East Lothian

North Kelsey County Primary School, North Kelsey, Lincolnshire

North Kesteven School, North Hykeham, Lincolnshire

North Tawton County Primary School, North Tawton, Devon

Northampton School For Girls, Northampton

Northbridge House School, London NW1

Norwich School, Norwich, Norfolk

Notre Dame Senior School, Cobham, Surrey

Nunthorpe Primary School, Middlesbrough, Cleveland

Oakfield Junior School, Atherstone, Warwickshire

Oakham School, Oakham, Rutland

Oaklands Junior School, Crowthorne, Berkshire

Oaklands RC School, Waterlooville, Hampshire

Oaklands School, Acomb, North Yorkshire

Oakridge Primary School, Stafford

Old Buckenham High School, Attleborough, Norfolk

Old Palace School, Croydon, Surrey

Oldfield First School, Oakworth, West Yorkshire

Our Lady of Sion School, Worthing, West Sussex

Our Lady of Victories Primary School, Keighley, West Yorkshire

Our Lady's Convent School, Loughborough, Leicestershire

Overleigh St Mary's CE Primary School, Handbridge, Cheshire

Oxenhope CE First School, Oxenhope, West Yorkshire

Oxford Brookes University, Wheatley, Oxford

Packington CE Primary School, Nr Ashby de la Zouch, Leicestershire

Padgate High School, Padgate, Cheshire

Pakefield Middle School, Pakefield, Suffolk

Pantysgallog Primary School, Merthyr Tydfil, Mid Glamorgan

Parklands High School, Chorley, Lancashire

Parkroyal County Primary School, Macclesfield, Cheshire

Parkside Middle School, Cramlington, Northumberland

Parmiter's School, Garston, Hertfordshire

Patchway High School, Almondsbury, Bristol

Pate's Grammar School, Cheltenham, Gloucestershire

Pegasus First School, Blackbird Leys, Oxford

Penboyr VAP School, Llandysul, Carmarthen, Dyfed

Peniel CP School, Peniel, Carmarthen, Dyfed

Penistone Grammar School, Penistone, South Yorkshire

Pennington CE School, Nr Ulverston, Cumbria

Pent Valley School, Folkestone, Kent
Perth Academy, Perth
Perton Middle School, Perton, West Midlands
Pinewood School, Nr Swindon, Wiltshire
Pontefract CE School, Pontefract, West Yorkshire
Ponteland County High School, Ponteland,
    Northumberland
Poole High School, Poole, Dorset
Pope Pius X RC Comprehensive School, Wath Upon
    Dearne, South Yorkshire
Preston College, Fulwood, Lancashire
Prestwick Academy, Prestwick, Ayshire
Prior's Field School, Godalming, Surrey
Priors Wood JMI School, Ware, Hertfordshire
Putney High School, London SW15
Queen Elizabeth's Grammar School, Blackburn,
    Lancashire
Queen Elizabeth's High School, Gainsborough,
    Lincolnshire
Queen Elizabeth's School, Wimborne, Dorset
Queen Ethelburga's College, Ouseburn, North Yorkshire
Queen Mary's High School For Girls, Walsall, West
    Midlands
Queen's School, Chester
R A Butler Junior School, Saffron Walden, Essex
Radcliffe High School, Radcliffe, Manchester
Radley College, Abingdon, Oxfordshire
Rainham School for Girls, Rainham, Kent
Ratcliffe College, Ratcliffe on the Wreane, Leicester
Ravenscroft Primary School, Bracknell Avenue, Kirkby,
    Merseyside
Reading Blue Coat School, Sonning, Berkshire
Reading Girls' School, Reading, Berkshire
Redhills Combined School, Exeter, Devon
Redlands Junior School, Dorking, Surrey
Rednock School, Dursley, Gloucestershire
Reedness Primary School, Goole, East Yorkshire
Reigate Priory Junior School, Reigate, Surrey
Rhosgoch Primary School, Rhosgoch, Powys
Ribble Drive Primary School, Whitfield, Manchester
Richard Clarke First School, Abbots Bromley,
    Staffordshire
Rickmansworth School, Rickmansworth, Hertfordshire
Ridgeway Primary School, Chasetown, West Midlands
Ridgewood High School, Stourbridge, West Midlands
Ringmer County Primary School, Ringmer, East Sussex
River School, Worcester
Rivington and Blackrod High School, Horwich, Greater
    Manchester
Robert Gordon's College, Aberdeen
Rochester Grammar School for Girls, Rochester, Kent
Rossington High School, Rossington, South Yorkshire
Roundhay School, Leeds, West Yorkshire
Royal Park Primary School, Sidcup, Kent
RSPB Pulborough Brooks Nature Reserve, Wiggonholt,
    West Sussex
Ruffwood Comprehensive School, Kirkby, Merseyside
Ryde School, Ryde, Isle of Wight
Ryecroft Middle School, Rocester, Staffordshire

Sackville School, East Grinstead, West Sussex
Sacred Heart RC Primary School, Ashton, Lancashire
St Albans High School, St Albans, Hertfordshire
St Andrew's CE Primary School, Hove, East Sussex
St Andrew's RC First School, Blyth, Northumberland
St Anne's First School, Bewdley, Hereford and Worcester
St Anselm's RC School, Canterbury, Kent
St Aubyn's School, Woodford Green, Essex
St Augustine's Priory, Ealing, London W5
St Bartholomew's CE Primary School, Penn,
    Wolverhampton, West Midlands
St Benedict's RC School, Bury St Edmunds, Suffolk
St Bernard's Convent School, Slough, Berkshire
St Bernard's High School, Westcliff on Sea, Essex
St Bernard's School, Rotherham, South Yorkshire
St Christopher's RC Primary School, Codsall, West
    Midlands
St Ciaran's High School, Ballygawley, County Tyrone
St Clare's RC Primary School, Lache, Cheshire
St Edmund's Catholic School, Portsmouth, Hampshire
St Edmund's College, Ware, Hertfordshire
St George's School for Girls, Edinburgh
St Giles' and St George's CE Primary School, Newcastle
    under Lyme, Staffordshire
St Helen's School, Northwood, Middlesex
St Helen's JMI School, Wheathampstead, Hertfordshire
St Hilary's School, Alderley Edge, Cheshire
St James' and the Abbey School, West Malvern, Hereford
    and Worcester
St Joan of Arc Catholic School, Rickmansworth,
    Hertfordshire
St John Fisher RC High School, Harrogate, North
    Yorkshire
St John's RC Comprehensive School, Gravesend, Kent
St Joseph and St Teresa Primary School, Wells, Somerset
St Joseph's School, Kenilworth, Warwickshire
St Joseph's Secondary School, Derry City, Co.
    Londonderry
St Lawrence CE Primary School, Nr Telford, Shropshire
St Leonard's CE Junior School, Bridgnorth, Shropshire
St Leonard's Primary School, Stafford
St Louise's College, Belfast
St Luke's Primary School, Cambridge
St Malachy's College, Belfast
St Margaret Ward RC School, Tunstall, Staffordshire
St Margaret's Primary School, Crossgate, Durham
St Mary's Bluecoat CE Primary School, Bridgnorth,
    Shropshire
St Mary's CE Primary School, Prestwich, Manchester
St Mary's CE Primary School, Mucklestone, Shropshire
St Mary's CE Primary School, Runcorn, Cheshire
St Mary's County Primary School, Bridgwater, Somerset
St Mary's RC High School, Lugwardine, Hereford and
    Worcester
St Mary's RC Primary School, Bridlington, East Yorkshire
St Mary's School, Dover, Kent
St Mary's School, Shaftesbury, Dorset
St Mary's School, Bromsberrow, Hereford and Worcester
St Mary's School, Cambridge

St Maurice's High School, Cumbernauld, Dumbartonshire

St Michael's Catholic Grammar School, North Finchley, London N12

St Michael's RC Primary School, Whitfield, Greater Manchester

St Monica's RC High School, Prestwich, Greater Manchester

St Nicholas' RC High School, Hartford, Cheshire

St Oswald's School, Alnwick, Northumberland

St Paul's Catholic School, Sunbury on Thames, Middlesex

St Paul's School, Barnes, London SW13

St Paul's School, Haywards Heath, West Sussex

St Paul's School for Girls, Edgbaston, Birmingham, West Midlands

St Peter and Paul RC High School, Widnes, Cheshire

St Peter and St Paul CE Primary School, Chaldon, Surrey

St Peter's CE Primary School, Portishead, Avon

St Philip's RC Primary School, Nr Uckfield, East Sussex

St Pius X Primary School, Barrow in Furness, Cumbria

St Polycarp's Primary School, Farnham, Surrey

St Thomas More RC Comprehensive, Eltham, London SE9

St Ursula's Convent, Greenwich, London SE10

St Wilfrid's CE High School, Blackburn, Lancashire

St Wilfrid's Middle School, Blyth, Northumberland

Sale Grammar School, Sale, Cheshire

Sandbach School, Sandbach, Cheshire

Sandling County Primary School, Maidstone, Kent

Scamblesby CE Primary School, Scambelsby, Lincolnshire

School of St Helen and St Catherine, Abingdon, Oxfordshire

Seaham School, Seaham, County Durham

Shap CE Primary School, Shap, Cumbria

Shaw Wood Junior School, Armthorpe, South Yorkshire

Sheering CE School, Bishop's Stortford, Hertfordshire

Sheffield Hallam University, South Yorkshire

Shenfield High School, Shenfield, Essex

Shrewsbury School, Kingsland, Shropshire

Sidmouth College, Sidmouth, Devon

Silverdale CE School, Silverdale, Lancashire

Sir James Smith's School, Camelford, Cornwall

Skinners' School, Tunbridge Wells, Kent

Skipton Girls' High School, Skipton, North Yorkshire

Slough Grammar School, Slough, Berkshire

Solefield School, Sevenoaks, Kent

Solihull Sixth Form College, Solihull, West Midlands

Sound County Primary School, Nr Nantwich, Cheshire

South Birmingham College, Birmingham, West Midlands

South Greenhoe Middle School, Swaffham, Norfolk

South Hampstead High School, London NW3

South Hunsley School, North Ferriby, East Yorkshire

South Kent College, Ashford, Kent

Spalding Primary School, Spalding, Lincolnshire

Speyside High School, Aberlour, Banffshire

Springhallow School, Ealing, London W13

Springhill High School, Rochdale, Lancashire

Springvale Primary School, Cannock, Staffordshire

Stainburn School, Workington, Cumbria

Staining CE Primary School, Staining, Lancashire

Stanborough School, Welwyn Garden City, Hertfordshire

Stanwell School, Penarth, South Glamorgan

Stanwix Primary School, Carlisle, Cumbria

Stiperstones CE Primary School, Shrewsbury, Shropshire

Stockport Grammar School, Stockport, Cheshire

Stoke Damerel Community College, Plymouth, Devon

Stoke High School, Ipswich, Suffolk

Stokesley School, Stokesley, North Yorkshire

Stonehill JMI School, Letchworth, Hertfordshire

Stoneygate School, Leicester

Storth CE School, Nr Milnthorpe, Cumbria

Stratford Girls' Grammar School, Stratford upon Avon, Warwickshire

Stromness Academy, Stromness, Orkney

Styal County Primary School, Styal, Cheshire

Sudell Primary School, Darwen, Lancashire

Sunny Bank Junior School, Potters Bar, Hertfordshire

Surbiton High School, Kingston upon Thames, Surrey

Sutton Grammar School, Sutton, Surrey

Sutton High School, Sutton, Surrey

Sutton Valence School, Maidstone, Kent

Sutton in Craven CE Primary School, Sutton in Craven, West Yorkshire

Swanwick Primary School, Swanwick, Derbyshire

Swavesey Village College, Swavesey, Cambridgeshire

Sycamore Lane County Primary School, Great Stanley, Cheshire

Sydenham High School, London SE26

Tadcaster Grammar School, Toulston, North Yorkshire

Tain Royal Academy, Tain, Ross-shire

Taunton Preparatory School, Taunton, Somerset

Taunton's College, Southampton

Teesdale School, Barnard Castle, County Durham

The Arnewood School, New Milton, Hampshire

The Arthur Terry School, Sutton Coldfield, Birmingham, West Midlands

The Ashbeach County Primary School, Ramsey St Mary's, Cambridgeshire

The Ashford High School, Ashford, Middlesex

The Belvedere School, Liverpool, Merseyside

The Blue Coat School, Edgbaston, Birmingham, West Midlands

The Bollin Valley Ranger Service, Wilmslow, Cheshire

The Bradbourne School, Sevenoaks, Kent

The Buttsbury Junior School, Billericay, Essex

The Cathedral School, Chelmsford, Essex

The Clough Hall School, Kidsgrove, Staffordshire

The Commonweal School, Swindon, Wiltshire

The Connaught School, Aldershot, Hampshire

The Cornwallis School, Maidstone, Kent

The Edinburgh Academy, Edinburgh

The English Martyrs' School, Leicester

The Hayesbrook School, Tonbridge, Kent

The Helena Romanes School, Dunmow, Essex

The Henrietta Barnett School, London NW11

The Highfield School, Letchworth, Hertfordshire

The Hills Lower School, Putnoe, Bedfordshire

The Holgate School, Hucknall, Nottinghamshire

The Holy Family School, Keighley, West Yorkshire

The John Kyrle High School, Ross on Wye, Hereford and Worcester

The Judd School, Tonbridge, Kent

The King's School, Canterbury, Kent

The King's School, Macclesfield, Cheshire

The King's School, Tynemouth, Tyne and Wear

The Leys High School, Redditch, Worcestershire

The Leys Primary School, Dagenham, Essex

The Leys School, Cambridge

The Licensed Victuallers' School, Ascot, Berkshire

The London Oratory School, London SW6

The Malling School, East Malling, Kent

The Perse School for Girls, Cambridge

The Ratton School, Eastbourne, East Sussex

The Rickstones School, Witham, Essex

The Robert Smyth School, Market Harborough, Leicestershire

The Royal Hospital School, Holbrook, Suffolk

The Royal Quays Education Centre, North Shields, Tyne and Wear

The Royal School, Lansdown, Avon

The Thomas Aveling School, Rochester, Kent

The Toynbee School, Chandler's Ford, Hampshire

The Whitby County High School, Ellesmere Port, South Wirral, Cheshire

The Woodrush High School, Hollywood, Birmingham, West Midlands

Thirsk School, Thirsk, North Yorkshire

Thomas's Preparatory School, London SW11

Thorne Grammar School, Thorne, Doncaster, South Yorkshire

Thornhill Primary School, Nr Egremont, Cumbria

Thorpe House School, Norwich, Norfolk

Thorpe Middle School, Idle, West Yorkshire

Threlkeld Primary School, Threlkeld, Cumbria

Tiffin Girls' School, Kingston upon Thames, Surrey

Tiffin School, Kingston upon Thames, Surrey

Tilston Parochial School, Tilston, Cheshire

Torc High School, Glascote Heath, Staffordshire

Torquay Boys Grammar School, Torquay, Devon

Townley Grammar School for Girls, Bexleyheath, Kent

Townsend Primary School, Bucknall, Staffordshire

Treverbyn County Primary School, St Austell, Cornwall

Trevethin Comprehensive School, Pontypool, Gwent

Trewern Outdoor Centre, Hay on Wye, Hereford and Worcester

Trinant Junior School, Nr Crumlin, Gwent

Tring School, Tring, Hertfordshire

Trinity College, Carmarthen, Dyfed

Trinity School, Belvedere, Kent

Trinity School, Leamington Spa, Warwickshire

Truro High School, Truro, Cornwall

Truro School, Truro, Cornwall

Tudor Grange School, Solihull, West Midlands

Turnditch CE Primary School, Belper, Derbyshire

Tytherington High School, Macclesfield, Cheshire

Underhill School, Maidstone, Kent

Unicorn School, Richmond, Surrey

University College of Ripon and York St John, York

University College School, Hampstead, London NW3

University of Brighton, Eastbourne, East Sussex

University of Strathclyde, Jordanhill Campus, Glasgow

University of Sussex, Falmer, Sussex

Uplands Community College, Wadhurst, East Sussex

Upperby Primary School, Upperby, Carlisle

Ushaw Moor Junior School, Ushaw Moor, Durham

Verulam School, St Albans, Hertfordshire

Wade Deacon High School, Widnes, Cheshire

Wadham Community School, Crewkerne, Somerset

Wales High School, Sheffield, South Yorkshire

Wallbrook Primary School, Coseley, West Midlands

Walton Hall School, Eccleshall, Staffordshire

Walton High School, Walton on the Hill, Staffordshire

Walton Priory Middle School, Stone, Staffordshire

Warcop CE Primary School, Warcop, Cumbria

Warwick School, Warwick

Washington School, Washington, Tyne and Wear

Watergate School, Liverpool, Merseyside

Weatherhead High School for Girls, Wallasey, Merseyside

Wellingborough Junior School, Wellingborough, Northamptonshire

Wellington College, Belfast

Wells Cathedral School, Wells, Somerset

Welsh Harp Environmental Education Centre, London NW9

Wentworth Junior School, Dartford, Kent

West Cliffe County Primary School, Whitby, North Yorkshire

West Kirby Residential School, West Kirby, Merseyside

West Twyford Primary School, London NW10

Westfield Junior School, St Ives, Cambridgeshire

Westfield School, Watford, Hertfordshire

Westholme School, Blackburn, Lancashire

Weston Point County Primary School, Runcorn, Cheshire

Whetley Middle School, Bradford, West Yorkshire

Whippingham County Primary School, Nr East Cowes, Isle of Wight

Whitby Community College, Whitby, North Yorkshire

Whitchurch High School, Whitchurch, Cardiff

Whitfield County Primary School, Whitfield, Kent

Whittingham CE First School, Nr Alnwick, Northumberland

Whittington CE Primary School, Nr Oswestry, Shropshire

Whitton School, Twickenham, Middlesex

Whittonstall First School, Consett, County Durham

Whitworth High School, Whitworth, Lancashire

Wickersley Comprehensive School, Wickersley, South Yorkshire

Willesborough Junior School, Ashford, Kent

William de Ferrers School, South Woodham Ferrers, Essex

William Edwards School, Stifford Clays, Essex

William Howard School, Brampton, Cumbria

William Hutson Junior School, Burton on Trent, Staffordshire

William Parker School, Daventry, Northamptonshire

Williamwood High School, Clarkston, Renfrewshire

Willoughby CE School, Alford, Lincolnshire
Willows Primary School, Lichfield, Staffordshire
Wilnecote High School, Wilnecote, Staffordshire
Wilson's School, Wallington, Surrey
Wimboldsley County Primary School, Nr Middlewich, Cheshire
Wincle CE Primary School, Nr Macclesfield, Cheshire
Windmill Hill County Primary School, Runcorn, Cheshire
Winifred Holtby School, Bransholme, East Yorkshire
Winterbourne Junior Girls' School, Thornton Heath, Surrey
Withington Girls' School, Fallowfield, Manchester
Wix County Primary School, Nr Manningtree, Essex
Woldgate School, Pocklington, East Yorkshire
Woldingham School, Woldingham, Surrey
Wolverhampton Grammar School, Wolverhampton, West Midlands
Woodford County High School (Girls), Woodford Green, Essex
Woodhouse High School, Amington, Staffordshire
Woodhouse Middle School, Biddulph, Staffordshire
Woodkirk High School, Tingley, West Yorkshire
Worlingham Middle School, Nr Beccles, Suffolk
Worth School, Nr Crawley, West Sussex
Worth Valley Middle School, Keighley, West Yorkshire
Worthen Primary School, Shrewsbury, Shropshire
Worthing High School, Worthing, West Sussex
Wulfurn College of Further Education, Wolverhampton, West Midlands
Wycombe West School, Nr High Wycombe, Buckinghamshire
Wye Valley School, Bourne End, Buckinghamshire
Wyndham School, Egremont, Cumbria
Wyvern School, Eastleigh, Hampshire
Yardley Primary School, Chingford, London E4
Yardleys School, Tyseley, Birmingham, West Midlands
Ysgol Dyffryn Conwy, Llanrwst, Gwynedd
Ysgol Gynradd, Aberporth, Cardigan, Dyfed
Ysgol Penboyr, Llandysul, Carmarthen, Dyfed
Ysgol Peniel, Peniel, Carmarthen, Dyfed
Ysgol Teilo Sant, Llandeilo, Carmarthen, Dyfed
Ysgol y Gader, Dolgellau, Gwynedd

Geography Task Force members who returned Land Use – UK results

Val Banks, Ashford, Middlesex
A M Barton, Wolverhampton, West Midlands
P Bellingham, Gillingham, Kent
R Blake, Nottingham
Ken Bland, Market Harborough, Leicestershire
David Boardman, Durham
Rachel Bowles, London
Sheila Bradford, Manchester
Simon Brown, Colchester, Essex
Jim Bruce, Bonnybridge, Stirlingshire
Lorna Burgoyne, London
Roger Cady, Carshalton, Surrey

Gary Cambers, Leire, Leicestershire
Kate Campion, Much Wenlock, Shropshire
Russell Chapman, London
Elizabeth Chubb, Thame, Oxfordshire
Adrian Copley, Morpeth, Northumberland
G Copnall, Ashtead, Surrey
Margie Daniel, London
Caroline Davis, Sunningdale, Berkshire
A G Downs, Skipton, West Yorkshire
Ioan Dyer, Carmarthen, Dyfed
Alun Evans, Shrewsbury, Shropshire
J Filby, Bradford, West Yorkshire
Peter Fox, Derby
A Freeman, Lewes, East Sussex
The Goodman Family, c/o The Perse School, Cambridge
A A Graham, Sale, Cheshire
B Harris, London
Ralph and Marie Hebden, Sheffield, South Yorkshire
Ken Hedley, Frizington, Cumbria
Rachel Houlston, Hook, Goole, East Yorkshire
Tracy Howard, Broxbourne, Hertfordshire
Joy Ingram, Dundee
R Jones, Stone, Staffordshire
Jean Kirkley, Oxford
Jeremy and Jane Krause, Chester
Paul Machon, Arthingworth, Northamptonshire
K MacKay, Stirling
Margaret Mackintosh, Exmouth, Devon
Andrew Marshall, Sale, Cheshire
Stuart May, Aldershot, Hampshire
John McKeown, Leicester
Richard Morgan, Hereford
David Nash, Belfast
M Newsome, Saffron Walden, Essex
Mike Norris, Hereford
J L Oates, Bournemouth, Dorset
A Pakula, Milford Haven, Dyfed
Mike Pearson, Preston, Lancashire
Victor Popperwell, Lowestoft, Suffolk
Cynthia Ramshaw, Impington, Cambridge
Paula Richardson, Redhill, Surrey
Bill Riddell, Morecambe, Lancashire
Liz Rose, Chelmsford, Essex
Amanda Sidwell, London
Howard Smith, Aberdeen
Derek Spooner, Hull, East Yorkshire
Caroline Stoneham, Aylesbury, Buckinghamshire
John Tomlinson, Skipton, North Yorkshire
Lesley Webb, St Neots, Cambridgeshire
Tom Whaley, York
Heather Willimott, Glasgow
Alison Wilson, Perth
Dave Wilson, Birmingham, West Midlands
David Wraight, Dudley, West Midlands
J Yuill (D of E Group), Kinross

Appendix 3:
Timetable of events

compiled by Mike Morrish

This appendix presents a detailed chronology of the entire project.

1990–92 Contact is established between the GA Worldwise Quiz Committee and organisers of the National Geographic Society Geography Bee in the USA (the Bee is a focal point of Geography Awareness Week).

Aug 1992 Rex Walford, the Hon. Secretary of Worldwise Quiz, talks further with National Geographic Society organisers of the Geography Awareness Week at the IGU Congress in Washington.

Nov 1992 The idea of a British Geography Awareness Week is raised by the GA at the Council of British Geography, but the matter is deferred and left in the hands of the GA.

July 1993 Rex Walford and Mike Morrish of the GA Worldwise Quiz Committee act as question-setters for the first International Geographical Olympiad, organised by the National Geographic Society but held at the Royal Geographical Society in London.

Nov 1993 Mike Morrish accompanies the British IGO team to New York during the US Geography Awareness Week and has discussions with the GAW management team. Mike Morrish and Rex Walford raise the Awareness Week idea at GA Council; Council authorises a feasibility study.

Jan 1994 Rex Walford and Mike Morrish commission the feasibility study from Pam Calvert of Communications Management (the firm who had handled the PR for the International Geographical Olympiad with considerable success).

Apr 1994 Mike Morrish and Pam Calvert take part in discussions about a possible Awareness Week with GA branch reps at the GA Annual Conference at Oxford.

Jun 1994 The feasibility study is presented to GA Council. Costs of £50,000 are projected. Council, influenced by the recent Dearing revisions to the National Curriculum, agrees to go ahead with an Action (rather than Awareness) Week if sponsorship can be found. The primary sector seeks involvement.

Jul 1994 *Geographical Journal* publishes 'The land cover of Britain, 1930–1990' by Barr, Fuller and Sheail (all scientists at the Institute of Terrestrial Ecology), an article about national land-use surveys.

Sept 1994 Rex Walford visits Sheail and Fuller at Monks Wood to discuss the possibility of schools being involved in a 1990s national land-use survey.

Oct 1994 The Action Week Committee meets for the first time. Mike Morrish is elected Chair and Rex Walford Secretary. Plans for a national land-use survey and an Action Week are agreed. Mike Morrish negotiates with the Ordnance Survey, who agree to supply free maps to schools undertaking key squares in the survey sample.

Nov 1994 The ITE confirms its willingness to be involved in the survey organisation. Philip Kivell (University of Keele) is enlisted as adviser on the survey of urban areas. The title 'Land Use – UK' is decided on.

Dec 1994 The GA Council approves the detailed plans and timetable for the survey to take place in summer 1996. The Scottish Association of Geography Teachers (SAGT) and the Association of Geography Teachers in Wales (AGTW) are invited to take part. A high-quality sponsorship leaflet is designed and commissioned.

Jan–July 1995 A concentrated search takes place for major sponsors, and a budget of £71,000 is sought to cover the costs of materials, administration and a full-time Project Officer and Secretary.

Feb 1995 The National Steering Committee embarks on more detailed plans and develops a pilot survey. A logo and publicity leaflet are designed and prepared.

Apr 1995 A display at the GA Annual Conference at Lancaster announces Land Use – UK; schools are recruited for the pilot survey.

May 1995 Cambridge PGCE students trial the pilot-survey materials.

Jun 1995 The pilot survey is undertaken by 17 schools to test the practicability of the survey plans.

July 1995 The National Steering Committee hears that no sponsor has been found, despite several near misses. It decides to seek more volunteer help to staff the project and to continue planning, in hope …

Oct 1995 Internal GA discussions take place concerning the possible scaling down of the project and its finances. *GA News* carries an article about how (the imaginary) Herbertson High School undertakes the land-use survey and participates in Geography Action Week.

Nov 1995 The GA Finance Committee agrees to underwrite Land Use – UK and Action Week up to £30,000; it is decided to charge a registration fee to participating schools.

Dec 1995 The Survey Handbook is compiled. GA Council approves a new budget.

Jan 1996 Launch articles appear in all GA journals, together with recruitment forms.

Feb–May 1996 GA Headquarters staff process registrations, and Ralph and Marie Hebden allocate squares to participating schools. Participating schools receive the first mailing (basic survey documents).

Apr 1996 Three charitable trusts respond favourably to requests for financial help for the project and contribute a total of £15,000. There is a Land Use – UK display at the GA Annual Conference at Southampton. A training 'Masterclass' is held for survey leaders.

May 1996 Training meetings are held all over the UK. Participating schools receive the second mailing (including 'twinning' information and a copy of the ITE Land Cover Map).

Jun–July 1996 Schools carry out the Land Use – UK survey.

July 1996 Participating schools receive the third mailing (including a display poster and '101 ideas' for Geography Action Week).

Aug 1996 The Geographical Task Force carries out the survey on squares not taken up.

Aug–Oct 1996 The Results Team processes and analyses the returns at Monks Wood, Huntingdon.

Sept 1996 Participating schools receive the fourth mailing (including copyright information).

Oct 1996 A preliminary results leaflet is published and sent to schools (fifth mailing).

Nov 1996 The preliminary results are launched at the Royal Geographical Society.

Early 1997 Further results are obtained. This book is edited and published.

References and further reading

Barr, C. J., Bunce, R. G. H., Clarke, R. T., Fuller, R. M., Furze, M. T., Gillespie, M. K., Groom, G. B., Hallam, C. J., Hornung, M., Howard, D. C. and Ness, M. J. (1993) *Countryside Survey 1990: main report*, Countryside 1990 Series Volume 2, London: Department of the Environment

Best, R. (1981) *Land Use and Living Space*, London: Methuen

Champion, A. G. and Townsend, A. R. (1990) *Contemporary Britain*, London: Edward Arnold

Coleman, A. (1961) 'The second land-use survey: progress and prospect', *Geographical Journal*, **127**, 68–186

Coleman, A. (1977) 'Land use planning; success or failure?', *The Architects' Journal*, 19 January.

Department of the Environment (1990) *Comparison of Land Cover Definitions*, A report by the Institute of Terrestrial Ecology, London: Department of the Environment

Fuller, R. M. and Groom, G. B. (1993) 'The land cover map of Great Britain', *Mapping Awareness*, **7**, 18–20

Fuller, R. M., Groom, G. B. and Jones, A. R. (1994) 'The land cover map of Great Britain: an automated classification of Landsat Thematic Mapper data', *Photogrammetric Engineering and Remote Sensing*, **60**, 553–562

Fuller, R. M., Sheail, J. and Barr, C. J. (1994) 'The Land of Britain, 1930–1990: a comparative study of field mapping and remote sensing techniques', *Geographical Journal*, **160** (2), 173–184

Jellicoe, G. A. (1960) *Studies in Landscape Design* Volume I, Oxford: Oxford University Press

Jellicoe, G. A. (1966) *Studies in Landscape Design* Volume II, Oxford: Oxford University Press

Kepes, G. (ed.) (1956) *The New Landscape in Art and Science*, Chicago: Paul Theobald and Co.

Kivell, P. T. (1993) *Land and the City*, London: Routledge

Matless, D. (1992) 'Regional surveys and local knowledges: The geographical imagination in Britain, 1918–39', *Transactions of the Institute of British Geographers*, **17**

Office of National Statistics (1996) *The ONS classification of local and health authorities of Great Britain*, London: HMSO

Office of Population Censuses and Surveys (1991) *1991 Census: Preliminary Report for England and Wales*, London: HMSO

Rycroft, S. and Cosgrove, D. (1994) 'The Stamp of an Idealist', *Geographical Magazine*, October, pages 36–39

Rycroft, S. and Cosgrove, D. (1995) 'Mapping the modern nation: Dudley Stamp and the Land Utilisation Survey', *History Workshop Journal*, **40**

Stamp, L. D. (1948) *The Land of Britain: its use and misuse*, London: Longman (3rd edition 1962)

Stott, A. P. (ed.) (1993) *Countryside Survey 1990: summary report*, London: Department of the Environment

Index